SRI AUROBINDO ON SHAKESPEARE

SRI AUROBINDO ON SHAKESPEARE

K. D. SETHNA

SRI AUROBINDO ASHRAM
PONDICHERRY, INDIA

First edition 1965
Second edition 1991
Third impression 2010

Rs 70
ISBN 978-81-7058-236-6

© Sri Aurobindo Ashram Trust 1965, 1991
Published by Sri Aurobindo Ashram Publication Department
Pondicherry 605 002
Web http://www.sabda.in

Printed at Sri Aurobindo Ashram Press, Pondicherry
PRINTED IN INDIA

PUBLISHERS' NOTE

Annamalai University invited K. D. Sethna of the Sri Aurobindo Ashram and the International Centre of Education, Pondicherry, to deliver two talks at their Shakespeare Symposium on September 1-3, 1964. He gave the opening and the closing talks of this quatercentenary celebration of the poet's year of birth: "The *Dramatis Personae* of Shakespeare's Sonnets" and "Sri Aurobindo on Shakespeare." What was delivered in either case was a part of what had been actually written. For, both the themes had developed far beyond the needs of the occasion. We are presenting in full the development of the second subject, covering all the points lit up by Sri Aurobindo in the work of the Bard. The numerous insights and critical observations of Sri Aurobindo—here linked together by a commentary further expounding and applying them—may well be regarded as India's most significant contribution to the understanding and appraisal of Shakespeare's genius.

We thank Annamalai University for letting us include the portions which were delivered at the Symposium.

NOTE TO THE SECOND EDITION

A few corrections have been made and an Appendix added, containing two references overlooked in the First Edition.

Contents

1.

Sri Aurobindo the poet and Shakespeare ... 1; Sri Aurobindo the literary critic ... 4; the general approach to Shakespeare ... 5; Shakespeare's place in world-poetry: the three levels of first-class poets ... 6; Shakespeare and Goethe ... 9; the chief determinant of poetic greatness ... 10; culture and poetic excellence ... 10; the five kinds of poetic style ... 11; the fifth or supremely inevitable style ... 13; Shakespeare and Racine ... 15; the role of technique ... 17; undertones and overtones in a new sense ... 18; the roles of accent, stress and quantity in Shakespeare ... 21; affinity between Shakespeare and Sri Aurobindo ... 24; mirroring Nature and re-creating Nature ... 26; an Elizabethan Visvamitra ? ... 27.

2.

The different levels or planes of poetic inspiration ... 30; Chaucer and Shakespeare ... 32; Shakespeare, Milton, Shelley, Gray ... 35; Shakespeare's plane and Bacon's mentality ... 37; Hamlet and intellectuality ... 38; Shakespeare and Donne ... 40; Shakespeare's kinship with Kalidasa ... 43; their bent of mind ... 44; painting of minor characters ... 44; characterisation of women ... 45; two points in which alone Kalidasa is superior ... 46; Kalidasa's prose and Shakespeare's verse ... 48; the problem of Shakespeare the Man and the Poet ... 50; the Sonnets and the theory of the man and the *milieu* ... 51; the Sonnet-forms ... 51; influences on early Shakespeare ... 52; the nation-soul and the poet ... 53; England's nation-soul, the English language and Shakespeare ... 54; poets and Nature ... 56; the inimitableness of a great poet's style ... 58; the development of poetic genius ... 60; Shakespeare and Marlowe ... 60.

3.

The demands of the Drama-form ... 62; Shakespeare and the dramatist's work ... 64; the Middle Ages, the Renaissance and the spirit of Elizabethan Drama ... 65; the characteristics of Shakespeare the dramatist ... 67; Shakespeare and Browning as dramatic poets ... 69.

4.

The process of poetic inspiration ... 73; the intuitive expression of Shakespeare ... 74; nobility of style ... 76; Shakespeare's earlier and later styles ... 78; the greatest lines of poetry and their contexts ... 79; "overhead poetry" ... 80; its derivations or substitutes ... 82; richness and restraint in poetry ... 83; epic sublimity and romantic ... 85; bare and direct statement ... 86; Shakespeare and the Johnsonian critic ... 87; Shakespeare neither philosopher nor mystic ... 89; Shakespeare and overhead poetry ... 92; the *mantra* ... 93; Shakespeare's puzzling Sonnet ... 96; Blake's "Hear the voice of the Bard" and Pure Poetry ... 99.

5.

Shakespeare and Blake ... 102; the Future Poetry and its past anticipations ... 102; Shakespeare and Whitman ... 106; quantitative rhythm, free verse and Shakespeare's prose ... 108; the top reaches of Whitmanian free verse and Shakespeare's "ordered measures" ... 111; the spiritual principle of the Future Poetry ... 114; the Future Poetry, Sri Aurobindo and Shakespeare ... 115.

Appendix

Sri Aurobindo's earliest writing on Shakespeare ... 116; Indian architecture and Shakespeare's art ... 116-118.

1

Sri Aurobindo's spiritual and philosophical height is now universally acknowledged. His stature as either poet or literary critic is still insufficiently seen. But the few, who have plunged sensitively into his prolific poetry with a mind trained on all the elevations of English verse, have been moved to speak of his more than 50,000 lines of lyric, narrative, drama and epic in the same breath with the work of the greatest. In this year of the quatercentenary of Shakespeare's birth, such a comparison may lead to the shocked raising of many eyebrows. But surely the age of Bardolatry is gone; and when one reads the opening quatrain of a sonnet by Sri Aurobindo in the Shakespearean form—

> I made an assignation with the Night;
>   In the abyss was fixed our rendezvous:
> In my breast carrying God's deathless light
>   I came her dark and dangerous heart to woo[1]—

the vibrant glory of the inspiration may stir one to imagine Shakespeare turned Yogi and sonneteering about some cosmic Dark Lady of his—some Mystery of the depths at once terrifying and fascinating, whose human reflex he had once loved and hated:

> For I have sworn thee fair, and thought thee bright,
> Who art as black as hell, as dark as night.[2]

Again, take Shakespeare suffering pangs of absence from the beautiful youth he addresses as "Lord of my love"[3]:

> How heavy do I journey on the way...[4]
> What freezings have I felt, what dark days seen![5]

Then stir with him to the thought of "Devouring Time"[6]

> And barren rage of death's eternal cold,[7]

and to the challenge—

> Yet do thy worst, old Time: despite thy wrong,
> My love shall in my verse ever live young[8]—

as well as to the assurance to the object of his devotion:

> Your name from hence immortal life shall have.[9]

Now, might we not fancy that Shakespeare, completely spiritualised and running the hazards of the Integral Yoga to transmute "hours of dross"[10] into "terms divine",[11] is bearing with some hope of the inmost heart the absence of his "fair friend"[12] whom he calls "a god in love",[13] when Sri Aurobindo closes his own Sonnet? —

> I walk by the chill wave through the dull slime
>   And still that weary journeying knows no end;
> Lost is the lustrous godhead beyond Time,
>   There comes no voice of the celestial Friend.
> And yet I know my footprints' track shall be
> A pathway towards Immortality.

However, we are not celebrating here the 92nd birth-anniversary of Sri Aurobindo the Poet. So I shall resist the quotableness of his poetry—and ask to be forgiven for only a few more lapses. The very first of them is prompted by an echo of the last word "Immortality" of the quotation already made and by the fact that now it is Shakespeare himself Sri Aurobindo is speaking of. It is from another sonnet on the Shakespearean model, "A Dream of Surreal Science". He is mocking the scientific vagary that all the poetry or spirituality or conquering dynamism of Man the dreamer and doer is merely a matter of the body's chemistry. Sri Aurobindo begins, referring to both Shakespeare and Homer:

> One dreamed and saw a gland write *Hamlet*, drink
>   At the Mermaid, capture immortality;
> A committee of hormones on the Aegean's brink
>   Composed the *Iliad* and the *Odyssey*.[14]

If we are disposed to be ingenious, we may aver that the essential Shakespeare can all be treated in brief under the three aspects hit off by Sri Aurobindo in his two lines on him here.

The writing of *Hamlet* would stand for Shakespeare's finest and most far-reaching self-expression—the profound cry of the heart's rosy blood grown strange and baffled by reflection of the brain's grey cells. The drinking at the Mermaid would represent the poetic frenzy arising from intoxication with the life-force, from a constant touch on the founts of a vitality stimulated at the same time by what is human, what is elemental and what is mythic, the half woman and half fish and their harmonious whole of fantasy which the sign of the Mermaid connotes. The capturing of immortality would sum up not only an achievement but also the means to it. Shakespeare becomes—in the words of Thorpe in that enigmatic dedication to the *Sonnets*—"our ever-living poet" by catching in the language of life and death the thrill of some depth of being, where abide the immortal patterns of things, where knowledge is the perceiver's consciousness directly penetrating the perceived, the inward interchange of a manifold oneness, and where—to adapt slightly a pregnant phrase of Sri Aurobindo's—

Sight is a flame-throw from identity.[15]

Probably Sri Aurobindo himself would have looked askance at this indulgence of ours in ingenuity. He was a spiritual realist and would have insisited that even his own words should be taken for what they were meant to be. In Shakespearean exegesis he would also refrain from imaginative adventures that make out Shakespeare to be a philosopher all through and his last plays a poetic allegory of some mystical experience. Sri Aurobindo sees all the subtle forces at work within or behind Shakespeare; but he does not lose sight of the man through whose transcribing mind the divine afflatus found its way to our earthly air. In the midst of modern criticism which is often either too fanciful and flighty or else too word-bound, page-pinned and does not even allow us to speak of a Shakespearean character beyond the limits of a play's verbal or symbolic scheme, it should be a healthy as well as instructive pleasure to review briefly Sri Aurobindo on Shakespeare. All the more profitable should it be to do so because through his comments on Shakespeare we can have an inkling of the whole general insight and outlook of Sri Aurobindo the literary critic.

Perhaps an introductory sense of his broad approach is most relevantly caught from some observations in 1917 on an issue raised by the fine Irish poet and critic who had made his physical and spiritual home in India, James Cousins. After appreciating in very high terms much of this writer's *New Ways in English Literature*, he[16] hangs out a necessary red light of warning: "Some occasional utterances in this book seem to spring from very pronounced idiosyncrasies of its distinctive literary temperament or standpoint and cannot always be accepted without reservation. I do not myself share its rather disparaging attitude towards the dramatic form and motive or its comparative coldness towards the architectural faculty and impulse in poetry. When Mr. Cousins tells us that 'its poetry and not its drama will be the thing of life' in Shakespeare's work, I feel that the distinction is not sound all through, that there is a truth behind it, but it is overstated. Or when still more vivaciously he dismisses Shakespeare the dramatist 'to a dusty and reverent immortality in the libraries' or speaks of the 'monstrous net of his life's work' which but for certain buoys of line and speech 'might sink in the ocean of forgetfulness,' I cannot help feeling that this can be at most the mood of the hour born of the effort to get rid of the burden of its past and move more freely towards its future, and not the definitive verdict of the poetic and aesthetic mind on what has been so long the object of its sincere admiration and a powerful presence and influence. Perhaps I am wrong, I may be too much influenced by my own settled idiosyncrasies of an aesthetic temperament and being impregnated with an early cult for the work of the great builders in Sanskrit and Greek, and Italian and English poetry.... Again, it is not likely that the poetic imagination will ever give up the narrative and dramatic form of its creative impulse; a new spirit in poetry, even though primarily lyrical, is moved always to seize upon and do what it can with them—as we see in the impulsion which has driven Maeterlinck, Yeats, Rabindranath to take hold of the dramatic form for self-expression as well as the lyrical in spite of their dominant subjectivity."

Now we may begin our survey proper—with the exact place Sri Aurobindo gives Shakespeare in world-poetry. Quite a number of popular parallelisms are abroad. For instance, Kalidasa is called the Shakespeare of India. Or we hear people saying that what Shakespeare is to England Racine is to France. Or else we find Dante and Shakespeare perched on equal peaks and sometimes Goethe is set up as an Olympian above all. To pick my steps correctly through the clutter of comparisons, I once posed Sri Aurobindo with the portentous problem of ranking all the great names in their right order. It was a task hardly congenial to so flexible and many-sided a taste as Sri Aurobindo's, but he gave semi-flippantly a very illuminative answer.

Naturally, he was speaking only of the past and from his own acquaintance with the poets rather than from their public reputations. Thus he has nothing to say of the Persian Firdausi, author of the *Shah-Nameh*. Nor has he any appraisal of the Nordic Sagas. But he leaves out none whom he finds worthy of high rank in the languages with which he was familiar. Apart from English which was like a mother-tongue to him because of his stay in England from his seventh to his twenty-first year, he knew, among the European languages, Greek, Latin, Italian, French, German, something of Spanish and, among the Asian, Sanskrit and many of the modern Indian vernaculars. In judging the literature of these tongues he brought four criteria: imaginative originality, expressive power, creative genius, scope of subject-matter, the last criterion implying also scale of work. A poet, as a whole, stands higher or lower according as he satisfies these criteria in a greater or smaller measure.

In order not to misunderstand Sri Aurobindo we should realise that a poet may be excellent in essential quality and yet may not stand high in the general Aurobindonian scheme because of an insufficient amount of work, insufficient quantity of essential quality. It is, of course, evident that the poet who has become famous just by that line on the old excavated city of Petra in the Middle East—

A rose-red city half as old as time—

cannot rank beside a writer like Gerard Manley Hopkins who has not only the celebrated evocation of Oxford—

Towery city and branchy between towers—

but also several other masterpieces of physical or psychological vividness. Yet Hopkins too is not large enough in his poetic production. Even Wordsworth and Shelley and Keats—names echoed by every literary scholar's heartbeats—are somewhat wanting in sheer bulk of beauty, if not also in a few other desiderata.

Sri Aurobindo[17] chooses eleven poets for the utter first class, but even these he distributes into three rows. In the top row he puts no more than four on an equal basis of essential excellence: Valmiki, Vyasa, Homer and Shakespeare.

In the second row come Dante, Kalidasa, Aeschylus, Sophocles, Virgil and Milton, their places in the series indicating more or less their merit.

In the third row stands in solitary grandeur Goethe.

Those in the first have to a supreme degree all the qualifications. Those in the second are a little deficient in one matter or another. Dante and Kalidasa have the same imaginative originality and expressive power as the very first four; they have also a wide enough scope, a sufficient amount of work. But they lack the elemental creativity as of a demiurge that characterises Valmiki, Vyasa, Homer and Shakespeare. They have, instead, built their worlds and peopled them by an energetic constructiveness of the poetic mind's vision. Aeschylus is a seer and creator, but his scale is much smaller: almost the same can be said of Sophocles. Virgil and Milton command a still less spontaneous breath of creative genius. Although their expressive power is immense, where in their works do we meet with a teeming world like that of the Shakespearean plays or of the Sanskrit and Greek epics or even the more limited triple world of Dante, particularly his Inferno with its intensely articulated characters in various states of torture? Milton has his fallen archangel Satan coming alive and a few signs of individual animation in his Eve; Virgil has his heroic Aeneas and tragic Dido—but most of the other characters in the English as well as the Roman poet are hurried sketches instead of fully realised pictures. These writers "live rather by what they have said than by what they have made".[18]

Questioned on Goethe at a later time by a disciple who admired that German enormously and considered him as outstripping Shakespeare in profundity if not also in poetic originality, Sri Aurobindo[19], replied: "Yes, Goethe goes much deeper than Shakespeare; he has an incomparably greater intellect than the English poet and sounded problems of life and thought Shakespeare had no means of approaching even. But he was certainly not a greater poet; I do not find myself very ready to admit either that he was Shakespeare's equal. He wrote out of a high poetic intelligence but his style and movement nowhere came near the poetic power, the magic, the sovereign expression and profound or subtle rhythms of Shakespeare. Shakespeare was a supreme poet and, one might almost say, nothing else; Goethe was by far the greater man and the greater brain, but he was a poet by choice, his mind's choice among its many high and effulgent possibilities, rather than by the very necessity of his being. He wrote his poetry as he did everything else with a great skill and an inspired subtlety of language and effective genius but it was only part of his genius and not the whole. There is too a touch mostly wanting—the touch of an absolute, an intensely inspired inevitability; a few quite supreme poets have that in abundance, in others it comes by occasional jets or flashes."

Here we may clarify Sri Aurobindo's attitude to the scope or range of a poet's work. A poet, to sit in the very first row, must be great in his scope, his range; but all in this row need not be equals in that respect. The equality required lies elsewhere—in poetic values proper. "When I said there were no greater poets than Homer and Shakespeare,"explains Sri Aurobindo,[20] "I was thinking of their essential force and beauty—not of the scope of their work as a whole; for there are poets greater in their range. The *Mahabharata* is from that point of view a far greater creation than the *Iliad*, the *Ramayana* than the *Odyssey*, and spread, either and both of them, their strength and their achievement over a larger field than the whole dramatic world of Shakespeare; both are built on an almost cosmic vastness of plan and take all human life (the *Mahabharata* all human thought as well) in their scope and touch too on things which the Greek and Elizabethan poets could not even glimpse. But as poets—as masters of rhythm and language and the expression of poetic beauty—Vyasa and Valmiki, though not inferior, are not greater than either the English or the Greek poet."

Germane to the subject is also a question asked about culture. Sri Aurobindo[21] does not suppose that all-round culture has much to do with excelling in any art, but there can be for him a certain turn or element in the excellence which an all-round culture makes possible. He[22] writes: "Shakespeare's poetry, for instance, is that of a man with a vivid and many-sided response to life; it gives the impression of a multifarious knowledge of things but it was a knowledge picked up from life as he went: Milton's gets a certain colour from his studies and learning; in neither case is the genius or the excellence of the poetry due to culture, but there is a certain turn or colouring in Milton which would not have been there otherwise and which is not there in Shakespeare. It does not give any superiority in poetic excellence to one over the other."

Now we may concentrate on what Sri Aurobindo, when comparing Shakespeare and Goethe, means by "an absolute, an intensely inspired inevitability". The epithets in this phrase are important. For, Sri Aurobindo distinguishes five kinds of poetic style and, although all can reach inevitability, only one of the several possible inevitabilities deserves the honour of being called "absolute" or "intensely inspired". There is first the "adequate" style, which just covers the immediate simple impact of a thing and utters its suggestion in a language proper to it. We may cite the terminal couplet of Sonnet 87, lines which modern critics such as L. C. Knights[23] are inclined to praise because of their blend of yearning poetic diction with offhand colloquial immediacy. Recently Auden[24] has called this couplet "wonderful":

> Thus have I had thee as a dream doth flatter—
> In sleep a king, but waking no such matter.

Next is the "effective" or "dynamic" style: it responds in a more complex, more vibrant manner, catching something of the movement rather than the stance of its subject. A snatch from Hamlet's well-known soliloquy will serve to illustrate it:

>   To die, to sleep
> To sleep: perchance to dream: ay, there's the rub;
> For in that sleep of death what dreams may come
> When we have shuffled off this mortal coil,
> Must give us pause.   (III. i. 64-68)

The "illumined" style has a richer imagination, it seizes lights and shadows of significance that are not at play either in a thing's stance or in its movement but emerge by the pressure of an in-look at its psychology, as it were. We may draw upon *Cymbeline* for those phrases from Iachimo face to face with Imogen asleep:

>   the flame of the taper
> Bows toward her, and would under-peep her lids
> To see the enclosed lights, now canopied
> Under these windows, white and azure laced
> With blue of heaven's own tinct.   (II. ii. 19-23)

The fourth style is designated "inspired" in a special sense. All inevitable poetry is inspired and some of it which Sri Aurobindo picks out as absolute is intensely inspired, but, if we consider the word "inspiration" literally as "breath taken in", there is a quality in this fourth style which has to do with a certain extra purity as well as extra keenness of vibration, as if a rarefied air such as gods might breathe were blowing through it. It has not only an in-look but also an in-tone—a kind of spelled expression, at once elevated and subtle and poignant. Listen to the lines from *Macbeth*:

>   Duncan is in his grave;
> After life's fitful fever he sleeps well...   (III. ii. 22-23)

The whole final phrase, with its fricatives and sibilants and liquids, achieves a masterly much-in-little of meaning carried home to us in a harmony of words powerfully simple. Here is the "inspired" style at its finest. It is even doubtful whether it does not compass in a comparatively subdued key what Sri Aurobindo tells us is done by

12

another passage from the same play. After saying that all the four styles we have named can be raised to inevitability along their own line, he goes on: "The supreme inevitability is something more even than that, a speech overwhelmingly sheer, pure and true, a quintessential essence of convincingly perfect utterance. That goes out of all classification and is unanalysable. Instances would include the most different kinds of style."[25]

Before we mention the instances Sri Aurobindo picks out at a venture, we may submit some homely comparisons to stress the differences among the five styles enumerated. The adequate may be likened to a photograph in faultless focus. The effective or dynamic would be a motion picture. The illumined can be called a technicolour film. The inspired would then be a drama staged right in front of us. And the supremely inevitable would be pulsing palpable life itself, catching us up in multifarious incalculable patterns.

Sri Aurobindo's instances of this style are: Homer's descent of Apollo from Olympus, beginning "Bê de kat' Oulumpoîo karênon chôömenos kêr",[a] Virgil's "Sunt lacrimae rerum et mentem mortalia tangunt"[b] and "O passi graviora, dabit deus his quoque finem,"[c] Wordsworth's mind of Newton "Voyaging through strange seas of Thought, alone" as well as "The Winds come to me from the fields of sleep", Keats's "magic casements

---

a. "Down from the peaks of Olympus he came, wrath vexing his heartstrings" (Sri Aurobindo).

b. "Tears in the nature of things, hearts touched by human transience" (C. Day Lewis).

c. "Fiercer griefs you have suffered; to these too God will give ending" (Sri Aurobindo).

13

opening on the foam / Of perilous seas in faery lands forlorn" and the lines where Macbeth (who has also the title "Thane of Glamis and Cawdor") confides in his wife the hallucinated hearing of a voice in the wake of the terrible deed he has done against an innocent man lying helpless in his slumber:

> Still it cried 'Sleep no more!' to all the house:
> 'Glamis hath murdered sleep, and therefore Cawdor
> Shall sleep no more, Macbeth shall sleep no more!'
> (II.ii.43-45)

Sri Aurobindo considers this style of absolute inevitability as unanalysable. He means, according to me, that although it may have affinity to any of the other styles, in the turn of its vision and of its word, it breaks through the bounds of excellence possible to all of them by their own acmes. I do not think he means that we can give no analysis of the conditions under which it performs its expressive miracle in this or that example. In commenting on the passage from Homer he observes that the words describing Apollo's wrath and his quiver and the clang of his silver bow as he moved are quite simple, "but the vowellation and the rhythm make the clang of the bow go smashing through the world into universes beyond while the last words—'he came made like unto the night'—give a most august and formidable impression of godhead". So it may not be fatuous to search for some of the verbal and rhythmic means through which the essence of perfectly convincing utterance gets its super-distillation, its quintessentiality, in the Macbeth-passage.

Shakespeare has found for the highly original turn to

which he has subjected the idea of retribution a verbal scheme with a warp of repetition and a woof of variety, which combines both awe and bewilderment. While the large tone of "Sleep no more" stuns us by its recurrence, the different proper names "Glamis", "Cawdor", "Macbeth" perplex us and by yet meaning the same person multiply maddeningly the intensity of the curse pronounced on him. If only "Glamis" or either of the other two had been iterated, the accumulated power would not have been so colossal; now it seems as though the dooms of three separate persons were heaped together upon the head of one at the same time that we understand through knowing the identity behind the three names that the same individual has been repeatedly condemned. Further, the names are all majestic and answer back the dominant rhythms. The result is assonances and consonances reenforcing an intricate and fearful sonority which carries in it the omnipotence of some occult cosmos of avenging life-force risen up against Macbeth.

It is not only Goethe who is lacking in abundance of such masterpieces of the poetic moment. There is not much to match it in the works of other European poets after Dante. One may have noticed that not a single French name from any period stands in Sri Aurobindo's triple first class. I am sure the French people will never forgive Sri Aurobindo for omitting their Racine. When I brought up his name as well as a few others who had a fair amount of impressive work to their credit, he mentioned that those who had just missed entering the third row and might be added on in a supplementary list were the Roman Lucretius, the Greek Euripides, the Spanish Calderon, the French Corneille and Hugo, the English

15

Spenser. This must be quite a blow to the French brain (or is it heart?) that would put Racine at the very top of all poetry. But, of course, the French have avenged themselves in advance on Sri Aurobindo for making so much of Shakespeare and sparing not even a side-look at their darling. Do we not know that Voltaire dubbed Shakespeare a drunken barbarian and congratulated himself on his own wide and penetrative taste when he published some selections from Shakespeare as rare pearls salvaged from a huge dunghill? Perhaps many do not know what Napoleon said. Napoleon who thought "impossible" a word found only in the dictionary of fools forgot himself and made the remark: "It is impossible to finish reading any of Shakespeare's plays."

But why does Sri Aurobindo let Racine come nowhere near Shakespeare? Here a cardinal principle of literary judgment is involved. For the problem of greatness and beauty arises. Sri Aurobindo has written: "In poetry greatness must, no doubt, be beautiful in the wider and deeper sense of beauty to be poetry, but the beautiful is not always great...I said...that art in the sense of perfect mastery of technique, perfect expression in word and sound was not everything and greatness and beauty of substance of the poetry entered into the reckoning. It might be said of Shakespeare that he was not predominantly an artist but rather a great creator, even though he has an art of his own, especially of dramatic architecture and copious ornament; but his work is far from being always perfect. In Racine, on the other hand, there is an unfailing perfection; Racine is the complete poetic artist. But if comparisons are to be made, Shakespeare's must be pronounced to be the greater poetry, greater in the vastness of its range, in its abundant creativeness, in its dramatic height and power, in the richness of his inspiration , in his world-view, in the peaks to which he rises and the depths which he plumbs—even though he sinks to fllatnesses which Racine would have abhorred—and generally a glory of God's making which is marvellous and unique. Racine has his heights and depths and widenesses, but nothing like this; he has not in him the poetic superman, he does not touch the superhuman level of creation. But all this is mainly a matter of substance and also of height and greatness in language, not of impeccable beauty and perfection of diction and rhythm which ought tò rank higher on the principle of art for art's sake."[26]

Aware of Sri Aurobindo's observations on the vowellation and the rhythm of Homer's passage on Apollo's descent from Olympus, we can never suspect Sri Aurobindo of playing down the role of technique. Discussing how in the supreme poetic speech there is an unusual bringing together of words and sounds with a power to plant within us a new unexpected meaning deeper than thought and defying translation into another language, Sri Aurobindo mentions the second line of Hamlet's dying words:

> Absent thee from felicity a while,
> And in this harsh world draw thy breath in pain...
> (V.ii.361-362)

"If you note," he says, "the combination of words and sounds in Shakespeare's line, so arranged as to force on the mind and still more on the subtle nerves and sense the utter absoluteness of the difficulty and pain of living for

17

the soul that has awakened to the misery of the world, you can see how this technique works."[27] But elsewhere he also tells us of this pair of lines: "Shakespeare's lines have a skilful and consummate rhythm and word-combination, but this gets its full value as the perfect embodiment of a profound and moving significance, the expression in a few lines of a whole range of human world-experience."[28]

The supreme poetry, we may generalise, is man's soul finding tongue for any aspect of its world-experience in a pattern of language where profundity acquires a perfect resonance. Then we get a verbal music in which the creative mood gets an accurate inward echo instead of an accomplished outward one. There is a musical perfection of outward poetry and there is a perfect music of poetry that is inward. The distinction has nothing to do with having outward or inward matter and theme. One can deal outwardly with inward things and *vice versa*. Even in the inward treatment there is a difference between sharp thought at work and keen sight as well as sensation communicating themselves. Of course, there are degrees of such sight and sensation, but whenever they are at play we have a musical perfection of inward poetry. Sri Aurobindo uses the terms "undertone" and "overtone" to characterise this poetic type and to distinguish within it two varying qualities. He has not expounded the subject: it comes into a letter to a disciple and he has just offered a few examples, but perhaps practical illustration is better than exposition and on the strength of it we may draw a few conclusions.

Ordinarily, the word "undertone" is used in poetic criticism to connote a mood or attitude running subtly beneath the open intention or drift. Thus in the lines of

18

Sonnet 86 about the Rival Poet—

> Was it his spirit, by spirits taught to write
> Above a mortal pitch, that struck me dead?— (5-6)

which ostensibly pay a compliment we may feel an ironical or satirical undertone, the very hyperbole serving secretly as an instrument of ridicule. Again, the line in Sonnet 73—

> Bare ruined choirs where late the sweet birds sang— (4)

which pictures leafless trees empty of birds in chilly weather is particularly opulent in overtone, evoking as it does in the mind of the scholarly reader images of the many cathedrals and churches whose choirs, once rich with beautiful ornaments and hangings and filled with singing boys in a row, were stripped and left deserted under the Protestant Tudors, Henry VIII and Elizabeth. Sri Aurobindo does not negate the ordinary usage of "undertone" and "overtone", but he brings a new sensitive appreciation of rhythmic psychology.

He writes: "there is a metrical rhythm, which belongs to the skilful use of metre—any good poet can manage that; but besides that there is a music which rises up into that of the rhythm or a music that underlies it, carries it as it were as the movement of the water carries the movement of a boat. They can both exist together in the same line, but it is more a matter of the inner than the outer ear and I am afraid I can't define further. To go into the subject would mean a long essay. But to give examples—

> Journeys end in lovers' meeting
> Every wise man's son doth know,

is excellent metrical rhythm, but there are no overtones and undertones. In

> Golden lads and girls all must
> As chimney-sweepers come to dust

there is a beginning of undertone, but no overtone, while the 'Take, O take those lips away' (the whole lyric) is all overtones. Again

> Friends, Romans, countrymen, lend me your ears;
> I come to bury Caesar, not to praise him

has admirable rhythm, but there are no overtones or undertones. But

> In maiden meditation fancy-free

has beautiful running undertones, while

> In the dark backward and abysm of Time

is all overtones, and

> Absent thee from felicity a while,
> And in this harsh world draw thy breath in pain

is all overtones and undertones together. I don't suppose this will make you much wiser, but it is all I can do for you at present." (11.5.1937)[29]

Whether the examples left the disciple much wiser or not, they must have made him feel the need to develop what Sri Aurobindo calls "the inner ear" and they must have caused him to wonder how Sri Aurobindo brought out all his examples from Shakespeare as if the Elizabethan dramatist were an "affable familiar ghost"[30] to him, though far indeed from "gulling" him in any way except in the sense that, according to Shakespeare himself, "The truest poetry is the most feigning."[31] In Shakespeare, "feigning", of course, has the archaic meaning of "fiction", and only suggests, as he puts it in a passage never stale with quotation, that the cardinal quality of poetry is the play of imagination. The passage is from *A Midsummer Night's Dream* (V.i.7-17) and is of particular interest because Sri Aurobindo has chosen it to illustrate in detail how inherent quantity—the length or the brevity of the time taken to speak a syllable's vowel—combines most effectively with distribution of stress, which is the vertical hammer-stroke recognised in English prosody as the living metre-builder within a more or less mechanical system of accentual high pitch and low pitch that are a very important element in the intonation of English. Quantity, the fundamental factor in the prosody of ancient languages like Greek, Latin, Sanskrit, enters the accepted English rhythm to give variety, subtlety, deeper significance. Sri Aurobindo deals with the position and function of stress and quantity in the Shakespeare-passage before going on to frame his own theory of a true English quantitative metre and to embody the theory in various experiments, including an epic in hexameters, *Ilion*. We are not now concerned with this momentous venture. We shall note only how understandingly and with what sensitive perception Sri Aurobindo can treat the accentual pentameters of Shakespeare.

Here is the well-known passage, with Sri Aurobindo's

scansion and markings—the stress indicated by a vertical line, the long-vowel syllable by a horizontal one, the quantitative shorts and the mere accents left unshown:

The lún|atic, | the lóv|er and | the pōet,

Āre of | imág|inā|tion āll | compáct:

Óne sēes | mōre dév|ils than | vāst héll | can hōld,

Thát is, | the mád | man; the lóv|er, āll | as frán|tic,

Sēēs Hél|en's bēau|ty in | a brōw | of Ēgypt:

The pō|et's ēye, | in a | fíne frén|zy rōlling,

Doth glánce | from héav|en to ēarth, | from ēarth | to héaven

And, as | imág|inā|tion bó|dies fōrth

The fōrms | of thíngs | unknōwn, | the pō|et's pén

Tūrns them | to shāpes, and gíves | to āir|y nó|thing

A lō|cal há|bitā|tion and | a nāme.

Sri Aurobindo's comment runs:

"The first six lines of this passage owe much of their beauty to the unusual placing of the stresses and the long-vowelled syllables; in each line the distribution differs and creates a special significant rhythm which deepens and reinforces the outward sense and adds to it that atmosphere of the unexpressed reality of the thing in itself which it is in the power of rhythm, of word-music as of all music, to create. In the first line two pyrrhics separate the two long-vowelled sounds which give emphasis and power to the first and last feet from the narrower short-vowel stressed foot in the middle: this gives a peculiar rhythmic effect which makes the line no longer a mere enumerative statement, it evokes three different rhythmic significances isolating and locating each of the three pure Imaginatives in his own kind. In the second line a swift short movement in its first half slows down to a heavy prolonged movement in its second, a swift run with a long and tangled consequence; here too the expressiveness of the rhythm is evident. In the third line there are no fewer than four long vowels and a single pyrrhic separates two rhythmic movements of an unusual power and amplitude expressive of the enormity of the lunatic's vision and imagination; here too, short-vowel stress and intrinsic-quantity longs are combined no less than three times and it is this accumulation that brings about the effect. In the fifth and sixth lines the separative pyrrhic in the middle serves again a similar purpose. In the fifth it helps to isolate in contrast two opposites each emphasised by its own significant rhythm. In the sixth line there are again four long vowels and a very expressive combination of short-vowel stressed length with intrinsic long syllables, a spacious amphibrach like a long plunge of a wave at the end; no more expressive rhythm could have been contrived to convey potently the power, the excitement and the amplitude of the poet's vision. Afterwards there follow five lines of a normal iambic movement, but still with a great subtlety of variation of rhythm and distribution of quantity creating another kind of rhythmic beauty, a beauty of pure harmonious word-music, but this too is the native utterance of the thing seen and conveys by significant sound its natural atmosphere. This passage shows how much the metrically unrecognised element of intrinsic quantity can tell in poetic rhythm, bringing real significations into what would be otherwise only sheer beauty of sound; quantity is one among its most important elements, even though it is not reckoned in the constitution of the metre. It combines with stress distribution to give power and expressive richness to the beat or, as it has been called, the strokes and flicks of accentual verse."[32]

Now we may touch on the topic of Shakespeare as Sri Aurobindo's "affable familiar ghost". Sri Aurobindo once wrote in a letter to the effect that after he had passed a certain stage of Yogic development and broken out of the narrow limits of the individual consciousness which is mostly the human condition he felt little need to read books, including of course books of poetry. It was as if the whole wide world of the mind everywhere with its possibilities of truth and beauty were thrown open to his inward eye. But in another letter he wrote that, apart from his own poems which were unavoidably there, he had with him in his room no book of poetry except the works of Shakespeare.

At first glance this special consideration given to Shakespeare poses a query: "Is not the Elizabethan dramatist the poet *par excellence* of human life as it is in earthly nature although not without a glimmer of things in earth no less than in heaven which are undreamt-of in human philosophy? And is not Sri Aurobindo preoccupied with just these rare things and is not his gaze fixed on the Superhuman, the Divine, straining far beyond the concerns of common life and their myriad complications and contortions which make the angels weep but send Shakespeare into ecstasies of creative expression?"

The answer to our query is not difficult to find. Sri Aurobindo is that extraordinary type of Yogi whose aim is to reach up to the Superhuman, the Divine, in order to strike back upon life—strike back not with a lash of light urging man to renounce earth by a mighty mass-movement towards Nirvana but with a sort of super-Prospero's staff so as to awaken man to the possibilities of a divine drama on the stage of the world. Sri Aurobindo would re-create human life. And in that ideal he has certain general affinities with his favourite Shakespeare.

It is not only that human life recreated by Sri Aurobindo would best be apostrophised in those words of Miranda in *The Tempest*, provided we keep them clean of the unfortunate association a popular satire of Aldous Huxley has forced upon the most felicitous group among them:

> How many goodly creatures are there here!
> How beauteous mankind is! O brave new world,
> That has such people in't!   (V.i.182-184)

We have also to observe that for all the vileness and wickedness that Shakespeare's dramatic genius has pictured and plumbed there is a preponderance of the "goodly" and "beauteous" over the vile and wicked. As Alfred Harbage[33] tots up, out of 775 distinct characters in the 38 plays, "378 (49 per cent) are indubitably good, 150 (20 per cent) are good in the main, 106 (14 per cent) are bad in the main and 133 (17 per cent) are indubitably bad...." "These statistics demonstrate," as Dr. K. R.

Srinivasa Iyengar[34] tells us, quoting Harbage, how "the Shakespearian world is a place to meet fine people and many of them...." However, it is not mainly by the multitude of fine people that the genius of Shakespeare is affined to Sri Aurobindo's creative ideal. The affinity lies in the sheer demiurgic power of creation which the Elizabethan dramatist brings and in its result of something which goes beyond the crowd of men and women we jostle hour after hour. According to Sri Aurobindo,[35] whatever theory about his own art Shakespeare put into Hamlet's mouth he does not in practice merely "hold, as 'twere, the mirror up to nature". There is in him "a moved and excited reception and evocation" of life as seen in the external world and acted out from day to day. If we speak in terms of the mirror, it is not Shakespeare's poetry we must mention but Chaucer's. Chaucer, in his large narrative, mirrors "clearly, justly, with a certain harmony of selection and a just sufficient transmutation in the personality and aesthetic temperament",[36] the visible figures, incidents, feelings and characteristics of earth-existence. This existence remains indeed Shakespeare's field, but there is a more inward reaction to it. About Shakespeare and that field Sri Aurobindo[37] writes: "Life throws its impressions, but what seizes upon them is a greater and deeper life-power in the poet which is not satisfied with mirroring or just beautifully responding, but begins to throw up at once around them its own rich matter of being and so creates something new, more personal, intimate, fuller of an inner vision, emotion, passion of self-expression."

Sri Aurobindo then refers to the ancient Indian distinction between several strata or levels of Universal Being and brings in the two names used by the Rishis for the objective and the subjective aspect of this Being: Virat and Hiranyagarbha. As Sri Aurobindo[38] judges it, Shakespeare's is "not a drama of mere externalised action, for it lives from within and more deeply than our external life. This is not Virat, the seer and creator of gross forms, but Hiranyagarbha, the luminous mind of dreams, looking through those forms to see his own images behind them." And then Sri Aurobindo mentions the Vedic sage Viswamitra whom Indian tradition credits with creating a new heaven and earth in his sacred wrath against the curbs imposed by the god Indra. Sri Aurobindo continues: "More than any other poet Shakespeare has accomplished mentally the legendary feat of the impetuous sage Viswamitra; his power of vision has created a Shakespearean world of his own, and it is, in spite of its realistic elements, a romantic world in a very true sense of the word, a world of the wonder and free power of life and not of its mere external realities, where what is here dulled and hampered finds a greater enlarged and intense breath of living, an ultra-natural play of beauty, curiosity and amplitude."

It is proper that this literary feat of an Elizabethan Visvamitra should have fascinated Sri Aurobindo. But such a label for Shakespeare is at once apposite and paradoxical. Paradoxical because Shakespeare is lacking in that very spirituality which distinguishes the Vedic Visvamitra. His drama, as R. M. Frye phrases it in his recent *Shakespeare and Christian Doctrine*, is "pervasively secular" and, over and above failing to set us on the track of his religious convictions, fails to grant us any glimmer from him of genuine inquiry into problems of religion. Sri Aurobindo is well aware of this, yet the comparison with

Visvamitra is apposite even beyond the role of the Elizabethan dramatist as an arch-demiurge. Bearing in mind not only that role but also something else, which marks Shakespeare out from most other poets, Sri Aurobindo[39] writes: "It is needful in any view of the evolution of poetry to note the limits within which Shakespeare did his work, so that we may fix the point reached; but still within the work itself his limitations do not matter. And even his positive defects and lapses cannot lower him, because there is an unfailing divinity of power in his touch which makes them negligible."

The last remark of Sri Aurobindo's reminds us of Shakespeare's own famous maxim on Hamlet's lips:

> There's a divinity that shapes our ends,
> Rough-hew them how we will.   (V.ii.10-11)

This is a dictum whose spiritual substance the Vedic Visvamitra might himself have uttered. In Shakespeare it occurs as a lesson to be learnt from the fact that

> Our indiscretion sometimes serves us well
> When our deep plots do pall....   (V.ii.8-9)

It is a profundity almost in excess of the occasion, a sort of wonderfully intrusive saw. But in any case it is in Shakespeare a rarity—for three fundamental reasons. First, he is not a poet of the thinking mind proper. Second, his habitual interest is in our shaped ends rather than in the shaping divinity. Third, although his drama lives from within and more deeply than our external life, this depth explores itself not with an assured sense of the in-world and of its forces but with mostly a cue from external forms. These three reasons define in general what Sri Aurobindo calls "the limits within which Shakespeare did his work". We may look at them a little more closely through Sri Aurobindo's eyes before finally measuring in as exact terms as possible what is meant by the pronouncement: "an unfailing divinity of power in his touch."

2

Sri Aurobindo has spoken of "the evolution of poetry" and "the point reached" in Shakespeare. To realise what is meant by this evolution we may mark Sri Aurobindo's distinctions of sources and channels within the inspired consciousness that writes poetry as well as his gradations of the race-consciousness within which the individual poetic inspiration works.

"We take little account," writes Sri Aurobindo[1], "of the psychology of poetic genius and are content with saying that the word of the poet is the speech of the imagination or that he works by an inspiration. But this is an insufficient account; for imagination is of many different kinds and inspiration touches the mind at different levels and breaks out through different media before it issues through the gates of the creative imagination." The most common among the various psychological instruments of the poetic afflatus are named by Sri Aurobindo the subtle-physical, the vital and the mental "planes". Beyond these are the rarely exploited planes where the inwardness necessary to all poetry plunges or rises to the directly mystical and spiritual consciousness.

Since man is typically a mental being and Sri Aurobindo speaks of inspiration touching the mind at different levels, we should more correctly say that poetry usually comes from the subtle-physical mind or the vital mind or the intellectual mind. The last-named is the mind proper, the first two are the mind functioning through what we may broadly term "sense" and "heart" as distinct from "thought".

The subtle-physical, the vital and the mental planes to which these terms point may be more clearly distinguished by the uses to which the essential "fine frenzy" of poetry is put in its verbal manifestation. It may be used, says Sri Aurobindo[2], "to give a deeper and more luminous force and a heightened beauty to the perceptions of outward life or to the inner but still surface movements of emotion and passion or the power of thought to perceive certain individual and universal truths which enlighten or which raise to a greater meaning the sensible appearances of the inner and outer life of Nature and man."

The mystical and spiritual planes come into play "when the mind of man begins to see more intimately the forces behind life, the powers concealed by our subjective existence, and the poet can attempt to reveal them more directly or at least to use the outward physical and vital and thought symbol only as a suggestion of greater things."

Generally, the plane on which the individual mind operates is a reflection of the level at which the nation or the race lives—at least this mind's ultimate system of symbols answers to the realities most vivid at that level. The English nation, in Sri Aurobindo's view, has followed most clearly the natural curve of evolution in its poetry, and the individual poetic mind is carried with it on the whole, although that mind may have its shootings beyond it in extraordinary moments of personal uniqueness.

English poetry strikes with Chaucer the typical note of the subtle-physical plane of inspiration. It is not the grandest note possible on that plane, for Sri Aurobindo considers Homer too a poet of the subtle-physical. What is characteristic here is that "the eye of...man is turned upon the physical world about him, the interests of the story of life and its primary ideas and emotions; he sees man and his world only, or sees the other worlds and their gods and beings in that image also, but magnified and heightened".[3] With the emergence of the vital plane, man begins to intellectualise, but still on the same subject-matter: there is more introspection and what forces itself on his view when he turns inward is the desire-soul with its intenser sensations and passions and then life and the world are seen with a new quivering sensitiveness and colourful longing and tumultuous reaction. Shakespearean poetry is the typical expression of the vital plane at its most powerful.

We can compare the notes of the two planes by taking Chaucer in one of his supreme emotional effects—what seem to me the most pathetic lines a lover ever spoke, pathetic by a heart-breaking homeliness verging on naïveté. Troilus, madly in love with Cressida, sees on the coat of Diomedes the very gift he has made to her as the sign of his love. He says to her:

> Through which I see that clene out of your minde
> Ye hen me cast, and I ne can nor may,
> For all the worlde, within my hertë finde
> T'unloven you a quarter of a day.

Now listen to Othello expressing his love. He thinks Desdemona has been false to him, but he cannot change his heart—though it does drive him to kill her. Here he is giving tongue to his desperate attachment to her beauty:

> Excellent wretch! Perdition catch my soul,
> But I do love thee! And when I love thee not,
> Chaos is come again.   (III.iii.90-92)

Mark the energetic thrust of the language, the grandiose passion in the words. The same thrust, though a little less emphatic and also a little less verbally grandiose and with a more imaginative vein, we find in another speech of Othello:

> ...had she been true,
> If heaven would make me such another world
> Of one entire and perfect chrysolite,
> I'd not have sold her for it.   (V.ii.141-144)

Perhaps the contrast between the subtle-physical and the vital planes may be more sharp when we take not emotional effects but reflective ones. Here is Chaucer achieving a striking moment of high seriousness *vis-à-vis* human life in general:

> What is this world, what asketh man to have,
> Now with his love, now in his coldë grave,
> Allone, withouten any companye?

A general pessimistic judgment is here, pressed home with two simple observations hinting the sudden intense desolation of death after life's joy of intimate companionship. But there is still a naïveté here, though functioning in a masterly manner: we are made to see and feel tragically how things are in their immediate outward reality. And the style is an easy limpidity which, while deeply moving us, stands quite at variance with the power to shake up our sensations and tear at our emotional roots, such as Shakespeare wields in Macbeth's celebrated outburst on life:

> Tomorrow, and tomorrow, and tomorrow,
> Creeps in this petty pace from day to day,
> To the last syllable of recorded time;
> And all our yesterdays have lighted fools
> The way to dusty death. Out, out, brief candle!
> Life's but a walking shadow; a poor player
> That struts and frets his hour upon the stage,
> And then is heard no more; it is a tale
> Told by an idiot, full of sound and fury,
> Signifying nothing.   (V.iv.19-28)

This kind of vigorous many-motioned passionate language is beyond Chaucer: a complexity is present, yet no mere complexity differentiates the Shakespearean cry from the Chaucerian: this complexity is not a quiet one, it is tempestuous, a surge of wide waves, each wave leaping with a sharp zest and pushing its fellow and mixing with it to create a further movement: the imagery is dynamic and multiple. Chaucer's thought seems to trouble our inner being by putting, as it were, the outside of our reflective self into a painful posture. Shakespeare's does it by penetrating our reflective self to the quick, so that it suffers a sort of revelatory violence to its nerve-shot inside. In brief, the thinking life-soul and not the thinking subtle-physical soul is gripped.

But the characteristic Shakespeare is to be disclosed not only by pitting it against the characteristic Chaucer. We must now confront it with utterances of the thinking mind proper. In the post-Shakespearean period the English consciousness moved beyond the vitalistic grade to know life from a freer height, "get a clear detached idea of its workings,...and see with the calm eye of reason, to probe, analyse, get at the law and cause and general and particular rule of [man] himself and Nature."[4] In Milton it reached a new version of the intellectual lucidity, austerity and sublimity that had marked the Classical poetry of Greece and Rome. From that time onward, various phases and domains of the mind-soul at thought, now with a surface vigour, now with a deeply exploratory and complexly ramifying force, float into our ken. To perceive the difference of soul-note in the post-Shakespearean period, we may first attend to the typical turns and vibrations of Claudio's speech in *Measure for Measure* on death and after-life:

> Ay, but to die, and go we know not where;
> To lie in cold obstruction and to rot;
> This sensible warm motion to become
> A kneaded clod; and the delighted spirit
> To bathe in fiery floods, or to reside
> In thrilling region of thick-ribbèd ice;
> To be imprisoned in the viewless winds,
> And blown with restless violence round about
> The pendant world.   (III.i.116-124)

Now we may listen to the oration of Belial, one of Satan's followers in *Paradise Lost*:

>   Our final hope
> Is flat despair; we must exasperate
> The Almighty Victor to spend all his rage,
> And that must end us; that must be our cure,
> To be no more. Sad cure! for who would lose,
> Though full of pain, this intellectual being,

> Those thoughts that wander through Eternity,
> To perish rather, swallowed up and lost
> In the wide womb of uncreated Night,
> Devoid of sense and motion?

The concluding words recall "this sensible warm motion" of Shakespeare, but when the latter is lost the loser is "the delighted spirit" of passion and emotion, whereas here it is "this intellectual being" with its Eternity-wandering "thoughts" that will be "devoid of sense and motion". And the whole cast of language and rhythm is of the deliberative mind and not of the mind impulsive.

Sri Aurobindo himself has taken from the *Macbeth*-ouburst the nihilistic phrase at the end—

> Life's but a walking shadow,...
>   ...it is a tale
> Told by an idiot, full of sound and fury,
> Signifying nothing—

and set it over against "Shelley's voicing of a kindred idea of transience":

> Heaven's light for ever shines, Earth's shadows fly;
> Life, like a dome of many-coloured glass,
> Stains the white radiance of Eternity,
> Until Death tramples it to fragments.

Sri Aurobindo[5] comments: "The one has the colour of an intuition of the life-soul in one of its intense moods and we not only think the thought but seem to feel it even in our nerves of mental sensation, the other is the thought-mind itself uttering in a moved, inspired and illuminative language an idea of the pure intelligence." Sri Aurobindo[6] warns us that even when in Shakespeare there is ostensibly a judgment on life, an idea that appears to belong to the thinking mind in its own rights, there is really an upthrow from the emotional or sensational being.

The Shakespearean thought leaping out of emotion and sensation rather than intellect can be gauged also by being juxtaposed with Gray's eighteenth-century "gem":

> The boast of heraldry, the pomp of power,
>   And all that beauty, all that wealth e'er gave,
> Awaits alike th' inevitable hour:—
>   The paths of glory lead but to the grave.

The thought-mind is active here, not at considerable depth but in a sufficiently impressive fashion which renders the conception moving, yet the chiselled imaginative rhetoric stirs us to think poetically rather than setting "our nerves of mental sensation" to feel the poetic idea.

Shakespeare's specific life-force inspiration may be made to stand out by taking even a certain contemporary of his and putting him side by side with the dramatist. That contemporary is no less a figure than Francis Bacon whom several literary "sleuths" consider to have secretly penned the plays and used Shakespeare as a convenient façade. Unfortunately for these scholars, Bacon has left us some verse under his own name and we have just to hear it together with the *Macbeth*-lines in order to realise not only that Bacon was a mediocre poet but also that he functioned from a poetic plane quite unlike the Shakespearean. Here is how his short piece, entitled *Life*, starts:

> The world's a bubble, and the Life of Man
>   Less than a span:
> In his conception wretched, from the womb
>   So to the tomb;
> Curst from the cradle, and brought up to years
>   With cares and fears.
> Who then to frail mortality shall trust,
> But limns the water, or but writes in dust.

Everything here is a versifying vibration of the reflective mind—an arid sort of anticipation of eighteenth-century didactic and epigrammatic poetry. Not a trace of the *vivida vis* from the vital consciousness that breathes in any pronoucement on life and death we may pick out from the great dramas.

While we are about Bacon we may quote what Sri Aurobindo[7] says in another context—the discussion of "Sight" as "the essential poetic gift" which sets apart Homer, Dante, Valmiki, Kalidasa and others as poets of the top class, however different they may be within that category. Sri Aurobindo declares: "There is often more thought in a short essay of Bacon's than in a whole play of Shakespeare's, but not even a hundred cryptograms can make him the author of the dramas; for, as he showed when he tried to write poetry, the very nature of his thought-power and the characteristic way of expression of the born philosophical thinker hampered him in poetic expression. It was the constant outstreaming of form and thought and image from an abundant vision of life which made Shakespeare, whatever his other deficiencies, the sovereign dramatic poet."

"Have you forgotten Hamlet?" we may be asked. "Does not Hamlet address us from the intellect? Does he not strike, with an inspiration beyond Bacon, the Baconian note? Does not his speech think as masterfully as anything in the later poets?" Well, Sri Aurobindo's characterisation[8] of Hamlet in a letter is: "Hamlet is a Mind, an intellectual, but like many intellectuals a mind that looks too much all round and sees too many sides to have an effective will for action. He plans ingeniously without coming to anything decisive. And when he does act, it is on a vital impulse. Shakespeare suggests but does not bring out the idealist in him, the man of bright illusions." The phrase that Hamlet acts on a vital impulse is important. It points to the basic psychological power behind the keen reflective operation. And that power, the vital being, exhibits itself clearly in Hamlet's language. To realise a dissimilarity of strain in the very stuff of the reflective articulation we have only to compare Hamlet's

> who would fardels bear,
> To grunt and sweat under a weary life?   (III.i.76-77)

with Wordsworth's

> the heavy and the weary weight
> Of all this unintelligible world.

Wordsworth is speaking from the grey cells: they are changing the urgencies of an oppressed existence to philosophic values, they present deep feeling yet with a detached contemplative air. Shakespeare's Hamlet is speaking from his guts: they stir the brain only to render coherent an instinctive shout of recoil and rebellion. The feeling swirls up from the depths with a cutting and devouring power which does not easily allow whatever philosophic values it may have to stand with marked independence.

No, we must not mix up things. The life-force is not tied down to one formula of personality, it can figure forth intellectualism; but through all variations its basic tone can be caught. This tone may be most acutely disengaged by comparing Shakespeare to another contemporary of his, with whom nowadays he is always associated: Donne.

Scholars have traced a new mentality emerging in the last years of the sixteenth century. It is said to break with the old mellifluous, simple, non-analytic, assured style of Spenser and of the early sonneteers and show itself developing in Shakespeare's own Sonnets from their initial accent—

> From fairest creatures we desire increase,
> That thereby beauty's rose might never die[9]—

to an accent "critical, dramatic, satirical, complex, and uncertain", as Patrick Cruttwell[10] designates it, or as he sums it up in a word, "metaphysical", *à la* Donne at his best. An instance he provides from Sonnet 130. 11-12:

> I grant I never saw a goddess go:
> My mistress, when she walks, treads on the ground—

which "is exactly in the spirit and manner, the jaunty knowing commonsensical manner"[11] of Donne's

> Love's not so pure, and abstract, as they use
> To say, which have no Mistress but their muse.

Another instance is the end of Sonnet 146 "which is one of the very few passages in Shakespeare explicitly and traditionally theological in its conflict between body and soul ('Poor soul, the centre of my sinful earth')."[12] There is the advice to the soul to thrive by denying the body:

> Then, soul, live thou upon thy servant's loss,
> And let that pine to aggravate thy store;
> Buy terms divine in selling hours of dross;
> Within be fed, without be rich no more.
>   So shalt thou feed on Death, that feeds on men,
>   And Death once dead, there's no more dying then.

To this may be compared the sestet of Donne's tenth "Holy Sonnet" on Death's Impotency:

> Thou art slave to Fate, Chance, kings, and desperate men,
> Thou dost with poison, war, and sickness dwell,
> And poppy, or charms can make us sleep as well,
> And better than thy stroke; why swell'st thou then?
>   One short sleep past, we wake eternally,
>   And death shall be no more; death, thou shalt die.

The closes of the two poems are very near each other in their mode of expression and the last lines look even like mutual echoes. But, taking Donne as a whole, can we really equate him in plane of inspiration with "mature Shakespeare"?

Sri Aurobindo has not given a direct answer. But we may elicit a verdict from a letter he[13] wrote on Donne after seeing some of his "ingenuities": "It seems to me that Donne falls between two stools. The Elizabethan ingenuities pass because of the great verve of the life force that

41

makes them attractive. Donne's ingenuities remain intellectual and do not get alive except at times, the vital fire or force is not there to justify them and make them alive and lively. On the other hand he keeps to an Elizabethan or semi-Elizabethan style, but the Elizabethan energy is no longer there—he does not launch himself as Milton did into a new style suitable for the predominant play of the poetic intelligence. Energy and force of a kind he has, but it is twisted, laboured, something that has not found itself. That is why he is not so great a poet as he might have been. He is admired today because the modern mind has become like his—it too is straining for energy and force without having the life-impulse necessary for a true vividness and verve nor that higher vision which would supply another kind of energy—its intellect too is twisted, laboured, not in possession of itself." (28.2.1935)

What we can gather for our purpose is: (1) Donne, despite being stamped with something of the typical Elizabethan style, stands mostly outside the Elizabethan inspiration of the life-force; (2) he introduces the movement of the poetic intelligence without quite the language proper to that source of inspired poetry; (3) he is a sort of midway between the Shakespearean and the Miltonic planes of inspiration and, for all his effectivity, is often wanting in that impeccable self-expression which in different ways is Shakespeare's and Milton's.

Applying these conclusions to the "intellectualism" as of a Hamlet breathing out the "mysticism" of Sonnet 146, we may pronounce: "Shakespeare moulds with unrest of emotion and sensation a mystic substance intuited, with his usual vitality, from the plane of the poetic intelligence. The result is a complement or counterpart of the 'metaphysical' Donne-effect. It is a thesis, as it were, suggesting from its own depths the antithesis which is at once opposed to it and continuous with it— the antithesis which is mystic substance born of the poetic intelligence and moulding emotion and sensation with an unrest of ideative ingenuity and curiosity." In general we may affirm: "Not only is Donne lacking for the most part in the *vivida vis* of Shakespeare: he is also the intellect rather than the vital self in his basis, even if he is the intellect in a far more poetic drive than Bacon and nearer to mature Shakespeare than the pretty lifeless versifier of *Life*."

Here, with a "take-off" from the basic tone of the life-force which should be distinguished from all *à peu près* to it and recognised through all its variations, a short digressive flight would be in order. It would explain why Kalidasa, although not equal in dramatic poetry to Shakespeare, can be more properly labelled as the Shakespeare of India than Aeschylus or Sophocles as the Shakespeare of Greece, and Corneille or Racine as the Shakespeare of France.

According to Sri Aurobindo,[14] the Greek dramatists deal with life from the viewpoint of the inspired reason and the enlightened and chastened aesthetic sense, the French from that of the clear-thinking intellect and emotional sentiment. The creative intelligence, not the creative life-force, wrote their poetry, their plays. Piercing through the variations springing "from national difference, the cast of the civilisation, the cultural atmosphere, the individual idiosyncrasy", Sri Aurobindo is able to catch in Kalidasa and Shakespeare "some fundamental likeness of spirit". He[15] remarks: "Elizabethan poetry was the work of the life-spirit in a new, raw and vigorous people not yet tamed by a restraining and formative culture, a people with the crude tendencies of the occidental mind rioting almost in the exuberance of a state of nature. The poetry of the classical Sanskrit writers was the work of Asiatic minds, scholars, court-poets in an age of immense intellectual development and an excessive, almost over-cultivated refinement, but still that too was a poetry of the life-spirit. In spite of a broad gulf of difference we yet find an extraordinary basic kinship between these two very widely separated great ages of poetry, though there was never any possibility of contact between that earlier oriental and this later occidental work,— the dramas of Kalidasa and some of the dramatic romances of Shakespeare, plays like the Sanskrit *Seal of Rakshasa* and *Toy-Cart* and Elizabethan historic and melodramatic pieces, the poetry of the *Cloud-Messenger* and erotic Elizabethan poetry, the romantically vivid and descriptive narrative method of Spenser's *Faerie Queene* and the more intellectual romantic vividness and descriptive elaborateness of the *Line of Raghu* and the *Birth of the War-God*. This kinship arises from the likeness of essential motive and psychological basic type and emerges and asserts itself in spite of the enormous cultural division."

Because of that kinship a few comparisons between Shakespeare and Kalidasa, which Sri Aurobindo has made in some early writings, acquire special interest. First, as to bent of mind. Sri Aurobindo[16] says of Kalidasa: "Like Shakespeare...he seems not to have cared deeply for religion." Next, as to character-painting. "Nothing... distinguishes," declares Sri Aurobindo,[17] "the dramatic artist from the poet who has trespassed into drama than the careful pain he devotes to his minor characters. To the artist nothing is small; he bestows as much of his art within the narrow limits of his small characters as within the wide compass of his greatest. Shakespeare lavishes life upon his minor characters; but in Shakespeare it is the result of an abounding creative energy; he makes living men as God made the world, because he could not help it, because it was in his nature and must out. But Kalidasa's dramatic gift, always suave and keen, has not this godlike abundance; it is therefore well to note the persistence of this feature of high art in all his dramas."

Sri Aurobindo[18] has also the remark on the creative artist Kalidasa: "In nothing else does the delicacy and keen suavity of Kalidasa's dramatic genius exhibit itself with a more constant and instinctive perfection than in his characterisation of women." Then Sri Aurobindo[19] generalises: "Insight into feminine character is extraordinarily rare even among dramatists for whom one might think it to be a necessary element of their art. For the most part a poet represents with success only one or two unusual types known to him or in sympathy with his own temperament or those which are quite abnormal and therefore easily drawn; the latter are generally bad women, the Clytemnestras, Vittoria Corumbonas, Beatrice Joannas. The women of Vyasa and of Sophocles have all a family resemblance: all possess a quiet or commanding masculine strength of character which reveals their parentage. Other poets we see succeeding in a single feminine character, often repeating, but failing or not succeeding eminently in the rest. Otherwise women in poetry are generally painted very much from the outside. The poets who have had an instinctive insight into women, can be literally counted on the fingers of one's hand. Shakespeare in this as in other

45

dramatic gifts is splendidly and unapproachably first, or at least only equalled in depth though not in range by Valmiki. Racine has the same gift within his limits and Kalidasa without limits, though in this as in other respects he has not Shakespeare's prodigal abundance and puissant variety. Other names I do not remember: there are a few poets who succeed with coarse easy types, but this is the fruit of observation rather than an unfailing intuitive insight."

We may pause for a moment to complete the critical picture with a touch of statistics. Harbage, as we have mentioned, counted 775 "distinct" characters in Shakespeare's drama, but the actual number of character-creations is larger. It is 1,217—about half the number of "named" persons in the work of the greatest creative genius in literature after him, Balzac, whose *La Comédie Humaine* has 2,492 named and 566 unnamed characters. But it is noteworthy that out of Shakespeare's 1,217 no more than 157 are of the gentler sex. This proves how difficult it is for even a poet of the first rank to create and characterise women.

Now for a bit of surprise in Sri Aurobindo's treatment of Shakespeare and Kalidasa. So far Kalidasa, for all his dramatic genius, has stood inferior in Sri Aurobindo's eyes to Shakespeare. But in two points Sri Aurobindo[20] finds him overtopping the Elizabethan giant:

"Kalidasa's marvellous modesty of dramatic effect and power of reproducing ordinary, hardly observable speech, gesture and action, magicalising but not falsifying them, saves him from that embarrassment which most poets feel in dealing dramatically with children. Even Shakespeare disappoints us. This great poet with his rich and complex mind usually finds it difficult to attune himself again to the simplicity, irresponsibility and naive charm of childhood.

"Arthur, whom the Shakespeare-worshipper would have us regard as a masterpiece, is no real child; he is too *voulu*, too eloquent, too much dressed up for pathos and too conscious of the fine sentimental pose he strikes. Children do pose and children do sentimentalise, but they are perfectly naive and unconscious about it; they pose with sincerity, they sentimentalise with a sort of passionate simplicity, indeed an earnest businesslikeness which is so sincere that it does not even require an audience. The greatest minds have their limitations and Shakespeare's overabounding wit shuts him out from two Paradises, the mind of a child and the heart of a mother. Constance, the pathetic mother, is a fitting pendant to Arthur, the pathetic child, as insincere and falsely drawn a portraiture, as obviously dressed up for the part. Indeed throughout the meagre and mostly unsympathetic list of mothers in Shakespeare's otherwise various and splendid gallery there is not even one in whose speech there is the throbbing of a mother's heart; the sacred beauty of maternity is touched upon in a phrase or two; but from Shakespeare we expect something more, some perfect and passionate enshrining of the most engrossing and selfless of human affections. To this there is not even an approach. In this one respect the Indian poet, perhaps from the superior depth and keenness of the domestic feelings peculiar to his nation, outstripped his greater English compeer."

Sri Aurobindo[21] appends a small sequel to this ruling: "Kalidasa, like Shakespeare, seems to have realised the instinct of paternal tenderness far more strongly than the maternal; his works both dramatic and epic give us many powerful and emotional expressions of the love of father and child to which there are few corresponding outbursts of maternal feeling. Valmiki's Kaushalya has no parallel in Kalidasa. Yet he expresses the true sentiment of motherhood with sweetness and truth if not with passion."

Dealing with the problem of translating Kalidasa, Sri Aurobindo comes to the prose portions in Kalidasa's plays and they carry him once more to Shakespeare—but not to the portions of prose in him. This is the most striking and fascinating element in Sri Aurobindo's fine observations,[22] apart from the delightful breath they bring of his memory of the rural England he knew in the course of his early stay in that country for fourteen years:

"The prose of Kalidasa's dialogue is the most unpretentious and admirable prose in Sanskrit literature; it is perfectly simple, easy in pitch and natural in tone with a shining, smiling, rippling lucidity, a soft carolling gait like a little girl running along in a meadow and smiling back at you as she goes. There is the true image of it, a quiet English meadow with wild flowers on a bright summer morning, breezes abroad, the smell of hay in the neighbourhood, honeysuckle on the bank, hedges full of convolvuluses or wild roses, a ditch on one side with cress or forget-me-nots and nothing pronounced or poignant except perhaps a stray whiff of meadow-sweet from a distance. This admirable unobtrusive charm and just observed music (Coleridge) makes it run easily into verse in English. In translating one has at first some vague idea of reproducing the form as well as the spirit of the Sanskrit, rendering verse stanza by verse stanza and prose movement by prose movement. But it will soon be discovered that except in the talk of the buffoon and not always then Kalidasa's prose never evokes its just echo, never finds its answering pitch, tone or quality in English prose. The impression it creates is in no way different from Shakespeare's verse taken anywhere at its easiest and sweetest:

> Your lord does know my mind: I cannot love him;
> Yet I suppose him virtuous, know him noble,
> Of great estate, of fresh and stainless youth;
> In voices well divulg'd, free, learn'd, and valiant;
> And, in dimension and in shape of nature
> A gracious person; but yet I cannot love him:
> He might have took his answer long ago.[23]

Or again, still more close in its subtle and telling simplicity:

> Ol.   What is your parentage?
> Vi.   Above my fortune, yet my state is well:
> I am a gentleman.
> Ol.   Get you to your lord:
> I cannot love him. Let him send no more,
> Unless, perchance, you come to me again,
> To tell me how he takes it.[24]

There is absolutely no difference between this and the prose of Kalidasa, since even the absence of metre is compensated by the natural majesty, grace and rhythmic euphony of the Sanskrit language and the sweet seriousness and lucid effectiveness it naturally wears when it is not tortured for effects."

In the context of Kalidasa a final light on Shakespeare as well as on the question of approach to him remains to be shown. Remarking that Valmiki, Vyasa and Kalidasa, the three greatest names in Indian poetry, are to us, outside their poetical creation, names merely and nothing more, Sri Aurobindo[25] says in effect that it is actually very fortunate that we do draw such a blank when we apply to Kalidasa the historical method. He[26] illustrates his thesis from the case of Shakespeare:

"The individuality of Shakespeare as expressed in his recorded actions and his relations to his contemporaries is a matter of history and has nothing to do with appreciation of his poetry. It may interest me as a study of human character and intellect but I have no concern with it when I am reading *Hamlet* or even when I am reading the *Sonnets*; on the contrary, it may often come between me and the genuine revelation of the poet in his work, for actions seldom reveal more than the outer, bodily and sensational man while his word takes us within to the mind and the reason, the receiving and the selecting part of him which are his truer self. It may matter to the pedant or the gossip within me whether the sonnets were written to William Herbert or to Henry Wriothesley or to William Himself, whether the dark woman whom Shakespeare loved against his better judgment was Mary Fitton or someone else or nobody at all, whether the language is that of hyperbolical compliment to a patron or that of an actual passionate affection; but to the lover of poetry in me these things do not matter at all. It may be a historical fact that Shakespeare when he sat down to write these poems intended to use the affected language of conventional and fulsome flattery; if so, it does not exalt our idea of his character; but after all it was only the bodily and sensational case of that huge spirit which so intended,—the food-sheath and the life-sheath of him, to use Hindu phraseology; but the mind, the soul which was the real Shakespeare felt, as he wrote, every phase of the passion he was expressing to the very utmost, felt precisely those exultations, chills of jealousy and disappointment, noble affections, dark and unholy fires, and because he felt them, he was able so to express them that the world still listens and is moved. The passion was there in the soul of the man,—whether as a potential force or an experience from a past life, matters very little,—and it forms therefore part of his poetic individuality. But if we allow the alleged historical fact to interfere between us and this individuality, the feelings with which we ought to read the *Sonnets*, admiration, delight, sympathy, rapt interest in a soul struggling through passion towards self-realisation, will be disturbed by other feelings of disgust and nausea or at the best pity for a man who with such a soul within him prostituted its powers to the interests of his mere bodily covering. Both our realisation of the true Shakespeare and our enjoyment of his poetry will thus be cruelly and uselessly marred. This is the essential defect which vitiates the theory of the man and his *milieu*."

Before proceeding further we may make a small yet not insignificant parenthesis on the Sonnet-form. A novice in literary studies received from Sri Aurobindo[27] an account of the various interweavings of rhymes in this form, along with the remark: "The two regular rhyme-sequences are (1) the Shakespearean...and (2) the Miltonic.... The Shakespearean is closer to the natural lyric rhythm, the Miltonic to the ode-movement—i.e. something large and grave. The Miltonic is very difficult, for it needs either a strong armoured structure of the thought or a carefully developed unity of the building which all poets can't manage." To this we may pin a pendant from another letter:[28] "In a sonnet, thought should be set to thought, line added to line in a sort of architectural sequence, or else there should be a progression like the pressing of waves to the shore, with the finality of arrival swift in a closing couplet or deliberate as in the Miltonic form."

Now we may turn back to the topic of the historical approach and quote Sri Aurobindo[29] when he takes up for comment one particular side of this approach to Shakespeare: "We know from literary history that Marlowe and Kyd and other writers exercised no little influence on Shakespeare in his young and callow days; and it may be said in passing that all poets of the first order and even many of the second are profoundly influenced by the inferior and sometimes almost worthless work which was in vogue at the time of their early efforts, but they have the high secret of mental alchemy which can convert not merely inferior metal but even refuse into gold. It is only poets of a one-sided minor genius who can afford to be aggressively original. Now as literary history, as psychology, as part of the knowledge of intellectual origins, this is a highly important and noteworthy fact. But in the task of criticism what do we gain by it? We have simply brought the phantoms of Marlowe and Kyd between ourselves and what we are assimilating, and so disturbed and blurred the true picture of it that was falling on our souls, and if we know our business, the first thing we shall do is to banish those intruding shadows and bring ourselves once more face to face with Shakespeare."

Sri Aurobindo's early writings make a dead set at the *milieu*-theory. But his attack is against the pretentious exaggerative heart of it. He[30] is quite prepared to give the historical outlook and method their due: "I do not say that these things are not in a measure necessary but they are always the scaffolding and not the pile." And years later, though unrelenting towards the central claim of his old *bêtes noires*, he[31] wrote: "quite apart from its external and therefore unreal method, there is a truth in the historical theory of criticism which is of real help towards grasping something that is important and even essential, if not for our poetic appreciation, yet for our intellectual judgment of a poet and his work." This truth he[32] sums up:

"Generally, every nation or people has or develops a spirit in its being, a special soul-form of the human all-soul and a law of its nature which determines the lines and turns of its evolution.... All its self-expression is in conformity with them. And its poetry, art and thought are the expression of this self and of the greater possibilities of its self to which it moves. The individual poet and his poetry are part of its movement. Not that they are limited by the present temperament and outward forms of the national mind; they may exceed them.... But still the roots of his personality are there in its spirit and even his variation and revolt are an attempt to bring out something that is latent and suppressed or at least something which is trying to surge up from the secret all-soul into the soul-form of the nation. Therefore to appreciate this national evolution of poetry and the relations of the poet and his work with it cannot but be fruitful, if we observe them from the point of view not so much of things external to poetry, but of its own spirit and characteristic forms and motives."

From this we may deduce that to Sri Aurobindo Shakespeare could not have happened in any country except England. His surpassing qualities are the climax of attributes belonging typically to the English nation-soul and its language. That soul is not so marked in its characteristic form as the souls of other cultures, like the ancient Greek and Latin or the modern French. In fact, it is a combination of two soul-streams, and they are not easily fused. "We have first the dominant Anglo-Saxon strain quickened, lightened and given force, power and initiative by the Scandinavian and Celtic elements. This mixture has made a national mind remarkably dynamic and practical, with all the Teutonic strength, patience, industry, but liberated from the Teutonic heaviness and crudity, yet retaining enough not to be too light of balance or too sensitive to the shocks of life; therefore, a nation easily first in practical intelligence and practical dealing with the facts and difficulties of life. Not, be it noted, by any power of clear intellectual thought or by force of imagination or intellectual intuition, but rather by a strong vital instinct, a sort of tentative dynamic intuition. No spirituality, but a robust ethical turn; no innate power of the word, but a strong turn for action; no fine play of emotion or quickness of sympathy, but an abundant energy and force of will. This is one element of the national mind; the other is the submerged, half-insistent Celtic, gifted with precisely the opposite qualities, inherent spirituality, the gift of the word, the rapid and brilliant imagination, the quick and luminous intelligence, the strong emotional force and sympathy, the natural love of the things of the mind and still more of those beyond the mind, left to it from an old forgotten culture in its blood which contained an ancient mystical tradition.... From the ferment of these two elements arise both the greatness and the limitations of English poetry[33].... There are evidently two opposite powers at work in the same field, often compelled to labour in the same mind at a common production, and when two such opposites can coalesce, seize each other's motives and become one, the very greatest achievement becomes possible.... The greatest things in English poetry have come where the fusion was effected in the creative mind and soul of the poet[34].... And as a necessary aid we have the unique historical accident of the reshaping of a Teutonic tongue by French and Latinistic influences which gave it clearer and more flowing forms and turned it into a fine though difficult linguistic material sufficienly malleable, sufficiently plastic for Poetry to produce her larger and finer effects, sufficiently difficult to compel her to put forth her greatest energies."[35]

A brief digression on this point will be worth while. In a letter to a disciple Sri Aurobindo writes:"The English language is not naturally melodious like the Italian or Bengali—no language with a Teutonic base can be—but it is capable of remarkable harmonic effects and also it can by a skilful handling be made to give out the most beautiful melodies. Bengali and Italian are soft, easy and mellifluous languages—English is difficult and has to be struggled with to produce its best effects, but out of that very difficulty has arisen an astonishing plasticity, depth and manifold subtlety of rhythm.... I cannot agree that the examples you give of Bengali melody beat hollow the melody of the greatest English lyrists. Shakespeare, Swinburne's best work in *Atalanta* and elsewhere, Shelley at his finest and some others attain a melody that cannot be surpassed. It is a different kind of melody but not inferior."[36]

In Shakespearean drama the English language is thrown most triumphantly into "shapes at once of beauty and of concentrated power".[37] And in this drama the two sides of the national genius not only throw themselves out for the first time with a full energy but are welded into a unique phenomenon in which the exultant representation of action and character, passion and incident and movement is twinned with a lyric and romantic poetry of marvellous sweetness, richness and force.

The unique phenomenon is, of course, upon the vital plane which Shakespeare shares with Kalidasa among the world's dramatic poets. And while we are about coupling the two we may add a few further observations of Sri Aurobindo's in which they figure. Now it is in connection with Sri Aurobindo's discussion of Vyasa and his *Mahābhārata* in an early essay. He[38] writes on the dealings of various poets with Nature: "There are some poets who are the children of Nature, whose imagination is made of her dews, whose blood thrills to her with the perfect impulse of spiritual kinship; Wordsworth is of these and Valmiki. Their voices in speaking of her unconsciously become rich and liquid and their words are touched with a subtle significance of thought or emotion. There are others who hold her with a strong sensuous grasp by virtue of a ripe, sometimes an over-ripe delight in beauty; such are Shakespeare, Keats, Kalidasa. Others again approach her with a fine or clear intellectual sense of charm as do some of the old classical poets. Hardly in the rank of poets are those who like Dryden or Pope use her, if at all, only to provide them with a smoother well-turned literary expression. Vyasa belongs to none of these, and yet often touches the first three at particular points without defi-

nitely coinciding with any. He takes the kingdom of
Nature by violence. Approaching her from outside, his
masculine genius forces its way to her secret, insists and
will take no denial. Accordingly he is impressed at first
contact by the harmony in the midst of variety of her
external features, absorbs these into a strong retentive
imagination, meditates on them and so reads his way to
the closer impression, the inner sense behind that which is
external, the personal temperament of a landscape. In his
record of what he has seen, this impression more often
than not comes first as that which abides and prevails...."
As an instance of such an impression Sri Aurobindo[39]
quotes in Sanskrit a famous line, great and sombre,
striking the keynote of gloom and loneliness,[a] whose
English poetic translation he gives:

> A void tremendous forest thundering
> With crickets.

A second rendering of it in poetry occurs, many years
afterwards, woven into Sri Aurobindo's own *Savitri*:

> some lone tremendous wood
> Ringing for ever with the crickets' cry.[40]

Against Vyasa's brief and puissant touches, Shakespeare,
with his "strong sensuous grasp by virtue of a ripe,
sometimes an over-ripe delight in beauty", may perhaps
be set over with the opening lines of Sonnet 73 where the
poet describes himself as aging:

> That time of year thou may'st in me behold

a. *Vanaṁ pratibhayaṁ śūnyaṁ jhillikāgaṇanināditam*

> When yellow leaves, or none, or few, do hang
> Upon those boughs which shake against the cold,
> Bare ruined choirs where late the sweet birds sang.

Sri Aurobindo touches once again on Shakespeare—now at greater length—as well as passingly on Kalidasa in pondering the problem of "mixture" in the *Mahābhārata*. He is discussing "the presence of two glaringly distinct and incompatible styles" in this epic. He[41] writes:

"In unravelling the *Mahābhārata*...the peculiar inimitable nature of the style of Vyasa immensely lightens the difficulties of criticism. Had his been poetry of which the predominant grace was mannerism, it would have been imitable with some closeness; or even had it been a rich and salient style like Shakespeare's, Kalidasa's or Valmiki's, certain externals of it might have been reproduced by a skilled hand and the task of discernment rendered highly delicate and perilous. Yet even in such styles to the finest minds the presence or absence of an unanalysable personality within the manner of expression would be always perceptible. The second layer of the *Mahābhārata* is distinctly Ramayanistic in style, yet it would be a gross criticism that could confuse it with Valmiki's own work; the difference as is always the case in imitations of great poetry, is as palpable as the similarity. Some familiar examples may be taken from English literature. Crude as is the composition and treatment of the three parts of *King Henry VI*, its style unformed and everywhere full of echoes, yet when we get such lines as

> Thrice is he armed that hath his quarrel just
> And he but naked though locked up in steel
> Whose conscience with injustice is corrupted,[42]

we cannot but feel that we are listening to the same poetic voice as in *Richard III*,

> shadows to-night
> Have struck more terror to the soul of Richard
> Than can the substance of ten thousand soldiers
> Armèd in proof, and led by shallow Richmond,[43]

or in *Julius Caesar*,

> The evil that men do lives after them,
> The good is oft interrèd with their bones,[44]

or in the much later and richer vein of *Antony and Cleopatra*,

> I am dying, Egypt, dying; only
> I here importune death awhile, until
> Of many thousand kisses the poor last
> I lay upon thy lips.[45]

I have purposely selected passages of perfect simplicity and straightforwardness, because they appear to be the most imitable part of Shakespeare's work and are really the least imitable. Always one hears the same voice, the same personal note of style sounding through these very various passages, and one feels that there is in all the intimate and unmistakable personality of Shakespeare."

We may make a brief return to Kalidasa and Shakespeare, with our *point de départ* in Sri Aurobindo's statement: "Crude as is the composition and treatment of the three parts of *King Henry VI*...." Sri Aurobindo is considering Kalidasa's early composition, *Seasons*, and, as with *King Henry VI*, remarks:[46] "We see his characteristic gift even in the immature workmanship and uncertain touch and can distinguish the persistent personality in spite of the defective self-expression." Then Sri Aurobindo stresses an aspect of the development of poets, which is often overlooked. We expect great poets to be perfect from the first and we wonder how a genius like Shakespeare could be a late bloomer. But Sri Aurobindo[47] tells us: "poetic genius needs experience and self-discipline as much as any other and by its very complexity more than most. This is eminently true of great poets with a varied gift. A narrow though a high faculty works best on a single line and may show perfection at an early stage; but powerful and complex minds like Shakespeare or Kalidasa seldom find themselves before a more advanced period. Their previous work is certain to be full of power, promise and genius, but it will also be flawed, unequal and often imitative. This imperfection arises naturally from the greater difficulty in imposing the law of harmony of their various gifts on the bodily case which is the instrument of the spirit's self-expression. To arrive at this harmony requires time and effort and meanwhile the work will often be halting and unequal, varying between inspiration expressed and the failure of vision or expression."

This passage leads us to understand how Marlowe who was born in the same year as Shakespeare—1564—had reached greater maturity when he died in 1593. It is often said that if Shakespeare had died so young, Marlowe would have bulked larger in the history of poetry. But now we can see that this was so because Marlowe's was a less complex poetic nature than his. And the comparative simplicity may be due partly to a radical difference in fundamental gift. Dramatic genius has a complexity much greater than any other and Shakespeare, unlike Marlowe, was indeed its acme. "In fact," avers Sri Aurobindo,[48] "Marlowe was not a born dramatist; his true genius was lyrical, narrative and epic. Limited by his inborn characteristics, he succeeds in bringing out his poetic motive only in strong detached scenes and passages or in great culminating moments in which the lyrical cry and the epic touch break out through the form of drama."

3

Now that in many ways we have exemplified as well as defined the stage which Shakespeare sovereignly occupies in the evolution of poetry we may glance at it in terms of the drama-form and against the historical background of his age and throw into relief the Shakespearean moment in its limitations no less than its powers.

What are the true demands of the drama-form? Sri Aurobindo has some extremely pertinent remarks, gathering up a great deal in a little space. "Dramatic poetry," he[1] writes, "cannot live by the mere presentation of life and action and the passions, however truly they may be portrayed or however vigorously and abundantly. Its object is something greater and its conditions of success much more onerous. It must have, to begin with, as the fount of its creation or in its heart an interpretative vision and in that vision an explicit or implicit idea of life and the human being; and the vital presentation which is its outward instrument, must arise out of that harmoniously, whether by a spontaneous creation, as in Shakespeare, or by the compulsion of an intuitive artistic will, as with the Greeks. This interpretative vision and idea have in the presentation to seem to arise out of the inner life of vital types of the human soul or individual representatives of it through an evolution of speech leading to an evolution of action,—speech being the first important instrument, because through it the poet reveals the action of the soul, and outward action and event only the second, important, but less essential, reducible even to a minimum, because by that he makes visible and concrete to us the result of the inner action. In all very great drama the true movement and result is really psychological and the outward action, even when it is considerable, and the consummating event, even though loud and violent, are only either its symbol or else its condition of culmination. Finally, all this has to be cast into a close dramatic form, a successful weaving of interdependent relations, relations of soul to soul, of speech to speech, of action to action, the more close and inevitable the better, because so the truth of the whole evolution comes home to us. And if it is asked what in a word is the essential purpose of all this creation, I think we might possibly say that drama is the poet's vision of some part of the world-act in the life of the human soul, it is in a way his vision of Karma, in an extended and very flexible sense of the word; and at its highest point it becomes a poetic rendering or illustration of the Aeschylean *drasanti pathein*, 'the doer shall feel the effect of his act,' in an inner as well as an outer, a happy no less than an austere significance, whether that effect be represented as psychological or vital, whether it comes to its own through sorrow and calamity, ends in a judgment by laughter or finds an escape into beauty and joy, whether the presentation be tragic or comic or tragi-comic or idyllic. To satisfy these conditions is extremely difficult and for that reason the great dramatists are so few in their number,— the entire literature of the world has hardly given us more than a dozen. The difficult evolution of dramatic poetry is always more hard to lead than the lyric which is poetry's native expression, or than the narrative which is its simpler expansion."

Sri Aurobindo[2] continues: "The greatness of a period of dramatic poetry can be measured by the extent to which these complex conditions were understood in it or were intuitively practised. But in the mass of the Elizabethan drama the understanding is quite absent and the practice comes, if at all, only rarely, imperfectly and by a sort of accident. Shakespeare himself seems to have divined these conditions or contained them in the shaping flame of his genius rather than perceived them by the artistic intelligence. The rest have ordinarily no light of interpretative vision, no dramatic idea. Their tragedy and comedy are both oppressively external; this drama presents, but does not at all interpret; it is an outward presentation of manners and passions and lives by vigour of action and a quite outward-going speech; it means absolutely nothing."

The last phrase of Sri Aurobindo's sends us at once back to the termination of Macbeth's soliloquy on life. There, after life has been compared to a walking shadow and a poor player in agitation on the stage, it is summed up as an idiot's tale "signifying nothing" with its "sound and fury". Was Shakespeare acutely aware of the state of drama in his day, presenting without interpreting, giving merely the "fury" produced by "vigour of action" and the "sound" set up by "a quite outward-going speech"? From Hamlet's instructions to the players we can see that Shakespeare disapproved of many theatrical practices. The criticisms are well directed. And Shakespeare himself in his maturity is careful not to "o'erstep the modesty of nature" by garish tints or by piling up extraordinary events. But when it comes to theorising on the positive side, Hamlet—as we have noted—wants merely the mirror held up to nature, "to show virtue her own feature, scorn her own image, and the very age and body of the time his form and pressure".[3] This is not what Shakespeare actually does: his is the creative and interpretative vision that Sri Aurobindo speaks of—a looking around and behind and beyond virtue and scorn and the very age and body of the time. Sri Aurobindo[4] writes in another context: "the poet's greatest work is to open to us new realms of vision, new realms of being, our own and the world's, and he does this even when he is dealing with actual things. Homer with all his epic vigour of outward presentation does not show us the heroes and deeds before Troy in their actuality as they really were to the normal vision of men, but much rather as they were or might have been to the vision of the gods. Shakespeare's greatness lies not in his reproduction of actual human events or men as they appear to us buttoned and cloaked in life,—others of his time could have done that as well, if with less radiant force of genius, yet with more of the realistic crude colour or humdrum drab of daily truth,—but in his bringing out in his characters and themes of things essential, intimate, eternal, universal in man and Nature and Fate on which the outward features are borne as fringe and robe and which belong to all times, but are least obvious to the moment's experience: when we do see them, life presents to us another face and becomes something deeper than its actual present mask."

That Shakespeare should have failed to perceive by the artistic intelligence, even when fulfilling, the essential dramatic aim, may partly be explained by the nature of the poetic frenzy let loose in Elizabethan England. Sri Aurobindo traces this first abundant freedom, found by the subdued spirit of poetry in the country whose one chief earlier voice was Chaucer, to the new light and impulse that came from the Renaissance in France and Italy. He[5] observes: "The Renaissance meant many things and it meant too different things in different countries, but one thing above all everywhere, the discovery of beauty and joy in every energy of life.... It is Hellenism returning with its strong sense of humanity and things human, *nihil humani alienum*,[a] but at first a barbarised Hellenism, unbridled and extravagant, riotous in its vitalistic energy, too much overjoyed for restraint and measure. Elizabethan poetry is an expression of this energy, passion and wonder of life...." With Hellenism we associate the poetry of the inspired reason: the wide-ranging and deep-looking conscious intelligence moulding masterpieces with a chaste grandeur, a literature that goes by the name of Classical and not Romantic. The rebirth of ancient Greece should have brought the classical drama "of which the method was some significant and governing idea working out its life issues..."[6] But, though the intellect of Europe was freed from the shackles laid upon it by the Middle Ages, what leaped first forward and with greater reaction against the prisoning past was the vital energy. "The Middle Ages," writes Sri Aurobindo,[7] "had lived strongly and with a sort of deep and sombre force, but, as it were, always under the shadow of death and under the burden of an obligation to aspire through suffering to a beyond; their life is bordered on one side by the cross and on the other by the sword. The Renaissance brings in the sense of a liberation from the burden and the obligation; it looks at life and loves it in excess; it is carried away by the beauty

a. Nothing human is alien to me.

of the body and the senses and the intellect, the beauty of sensation and action and speech and thought,—of thought hardly at all for its own sake, but thought as a power of life." Especially in England the effect on poetry, which is itself never fundamentally a movement of the pure intellect, was extra-liberative. Elizabethan poetry "is much more powerful, disorderly and unrestrained than the corresponding poetry in other countries, having neither a past traditional culture nor an innate taste to restrain its extravagances."[8] In Shakespeare's genius the intensity and the excess get transmuted into a magic of copious formation. Unlike his dramatist-contemporaries and their later imitators, he "does not need to lay violent hands on life and turn it into romantic pyrotechnics; for life itself has taken hold of him in order to recreate itself in his image...."[9] Taking his hints from the world about him, he pours out a never-failing novelty of living figures moving to action on a sea of revealing speech. "His dramatic method seems indeed to have usually no other intellectual purpose, aesthetic motive or spiritual secret: ordinarily it labours simply for the joy of a multiple poetic vision of life and vital creation with no centre except the life-power itself, no coordination except that thrown out spontaneously by the unseizable workings of its energy, no unity but the one unity of man and the life-spirit in Nature working in him and before his eyes. It is this sheer creative Ananda of the life-spirit which is Shakespeare; abroad everywhere in that age it incarnates itself in him for the pleasure of poetic self-vision...."[10]

Sri Aurobindo[11] goes on: "He is not primarily an artist, a poetical thinker or anything else of the kind, but a great vital creator and intensely, though within marked limits, a seer of life. His art itself is life arranging its forms in its own surge and excitement, not in any kind of symmetry,—for symmetry here there is none,—nor in fine harmonies, but still in its own way supremely and with a certain intimately metric arrangement of its many loose movements, in mobile perspectives, a succession of crowded but successful and satisfying vistas. While he has given a wonderful language to poetic thought, he yet does not think for the sake of thought, but for the sake of life; his way indeed is not so much the poet himself thinking about life, as life thinking itself out in him through many mouths, in many moods and moments, with a rich throng of fine thought-effects, but not for any clear sum of intellectual vision or to any high power of either ideal or spiritual result. His development of human character has a sovereign force within its bounds, but it is the soul of the human being as seen through outward character, passion, action, the life-soul, and not either the thought-soul or the deeper psychic being or the profounder truth of the human spirit. Something of these things we may get, but only in shadow or as a partial reflection in a coloured glass, not in their own action. In his vision and therefore in his poetic motive Shakespeare never really either rises up above life or gets behind it; he neither sees what it reaches out to nor the great unseen powers that are active within it. At one time, in two or three of his tragedies, he seems to have been striving to do this, but all that he does see then is the action of certain tremendous life-forces which he either sets in a living symbol or indicates behind the human action, as in *Macbeth*, or embodies, as in *King Lear*, in a tragically uncontrollable possession of his human characters...."

Sri Aurobindo[12] makes a sort of summing-up: "The future may find for us a higher and profounder, even a more deeply and finely vital aim for the dramatic form than any Shakespeare ever conceived, but until that has been done with an equal power, grasp and fullness of vision and an equal intensity of revealing speech, he keeps his sovereign station...."

According to Sri Aurobindo, the only poet in English who had a dramatic genius approaching Shakespeare's, though with a different motive-power, was Browning. He best represented the spirit of the modern age "in its temperament of curious observation and its aim at a certain force of large yet minute reality.[13] He "was eminently a poet of life observed and understood and of thought playing around the observation, as Shakespeare was the poet of life seen through an identity of feeling with it and of thought arising out of the surge of life".[14] He was also the poet *par excellence* of the close and detailed psychologising, which pervades the literature of the time and in which "the modern mind has left behind all the preceding ages".[15] Compared with its performance "all previous creation seems...poor both in richness of material and in subtlety and the depth of its vision; half the work of Shakespeare in spite of its larger and greater treatment hardly contains as much on this side as a single volume of Browning".[16] But the modern mind has an assertion of the subjective personality. A poet's attempt "to live in the thoughts and feelings of other men, other civilisations betrays itself as only the mutiple imaginative and sympathetic extension of the poet's own psychology".[17] "Shakespeare succeeds, as far as a poet can, in veiling himself behind his creatures":[18] he is so pulled up

69

into the world-wide Life-force that they are not personally and individually thought and imaged by him so much as beheld and represented by it with an impersonality, a universality which, while not quite annulling the typical mould of Shakespeare the instrument, achieves its dramatic purpose without that mould's intrusion. "Browning, though he seems to have considered this self-concealment especially admirable and the essence of the Shakespearean method of creation, fails himself to achieve it in anything like the same measure. The self-conscious thinking of the modern mind which brings into prominent relief the rest of the mental personality and stamps the whole work with it, gets into his way; everywhere we feel the presence of the creator bringing forward his living puppets, analysing, commenting, thinking about them or else about life through a variation of many voices so that they become as much his masks as his creations."[19]

This does not mean that his characters are mechanical or mere structures of ideas with some colour daubed on them. They breathe and pulse. They may not possess an all-round reality in space and time; but their brief and limited cross-sections have a keen psychological movement animating their outward stance and shape. Nor, despite Browning's display of moral preferences and judgments in even the posture and speech he gives to his characters, do they lack something of Shakespeare's gift of *lebensraum* in which to spread and develop and plead for themselves. For, to Browning of the nineteenth century as to Shakespeare of the Renaissance, existence calls from all sides, "nothing human is foreign to his research and pursuit, all enters into this prodigious embrace".[20] "In his mass of creation he can be regarded as the most remarkable in invention and wideness if not the most significant builder and narrator of the drama of human life in his time.... His genius is essentially dramatic; for though he has written in many lyrical forms, the lyric is used to represent a moment in the drama of life or character, and though he uses the narrative, his treatment of it is dramatic and not narrative as when he takes an Italian *fait-divers* and makes each personage relate or discuss it in such a way as to reveal his own motive, character, thought and passion. He does not succeed as a dramatist in the received forms because he is too analytic, too much interested in the mechanism of temperament, character, emotion and changing idea to concentrate sufficiently on their results in action; but he has an unrivalled force in seizing on a moment of the soul or mind and in following its convolutions as they start into dramatic thought, feeling and impulse. He of all these writers [of the nineteenth century] has hold of the substance of the work marked out for a poet of the age. And with all these gifts we might have had in him the great interpretative poet, one might almost say, the Shakespeare of his time. But by the singular fatality which so often pursues the English poetical genius, the one gift needed to complete him was denied. Power was there and the hold of his material; what was absent was the essential faculty of artistic form and poetic beauty, so eminent in his contemporaries, a fatal deficiency. This great creator was no artist."[21] His language, for all its immense range, consummate technique, cogency and efficiency, was "in its base...the language of a prosaist and not a poet, of the intellect and not the imagination. He could throw into it strong colours, has sometimes though too seldom a vigorous richness and strong grace, achieves often a lyric elevation, but they supervene upon this base and do not ordinarily suffuse and change it or elevate it to a high customary level. Much strong and vigorous work he did of a great and robust substance, won many victories, but the supreme greatness cannot come in poetry without the supreme beauty".[22]

In another place Sri Aurobindo suggests that the model of drama on which Browning worked contributed to impede his Shakespearean possibilities. The English poetic spirit "has allowed itself to be obsessed by the Elizabethan formula; for it has clung not merely to the Shakespearean form,—which might after due modification still be used for certain purposes, expecially for a deeper life-thought expressing itself through the strong colours of a romantic interpretation,—but to the whole crude inartistic error of that age. Great poets, poets of noble subjective power, delicate artists, fine thinkers and singers, all directly they turn to the dramatic form, begin to externalise fatally; they become violent, they gesticulate, they press to the action and forget to have an informing thought, hold themselves bound to the idea of drama as a robust presentation of life and incident and passion. And because this is not a true idea and, in any case, it is quite inconsistent with the turn of their genius, they fail inevitably".[23] Here Sri Aurobindo is thinking directly of Dryden, Wordsworth, Byron, Keats, Shelley, Tennyson, Swinburne (apart from his *Atalanta*). But he has also written: "imitation of the catching falsities of this model...explains the failure of even a mind which had the true dramatic turn, a creator like Browning, to achieve drama of the first excellence".[24]

4

We have already probed the intensity of revealing speech, running through Shakespeare's dramas, in terms of various styles as well as of different planes. Now we may consider its essential movement, the process by which it takes birth, the process commonly termed inspiration.

"What we mean by inspiration," Sri Aurobindo[1] has stated, "is that the impetus to poetic creation and utterance comes to us from a superconscient source above the ordinary mentality, so that what is written seems not to be the fabrication of the brain-mind, but something more sovereign breathed or poured in from above. That is the possession by the divine *enthousiasmos* of which Plato has spoken. But it is seldom that the whole word leaps direct from that source,...ordinarily it goes through some secondary process in the brain-mind itself, gets its impulse and unformed substance perhaps from above, but subjects it to an intellectual or other earthly change.... But also there is in us a direct medium between that divine and this human mentality, an intuitive soul-mind supporting the rest, which has its share both in the transmission and the formal creation, and it is where this gets out into overt working, discloses its shaping touch or makes heard its transmitting voice that we get the really immortal tones of speech and heights of creation. And it is the epochs when there is in the mind of the race some enthusiastic outburst or some calm august action of this intuitive power, intermediary of the inspirations of the spirit or its revelations, that make the great ages of poetry."

Here by "soul-mind" Sri Aurobindo does not point directly to a mystical element in the contents of poetry. The soul-mind can function through any part of our psychology and charge with its presence all poetry, be it openly mystical or no. Its common play, whatever its instrument, is what Sri Aurobindo terms "intuitive power". And by way of illustrating both how it acts and what is meant by a great age of poetry produced through its action, Sri Aurobindo[2] tells us: "In English literature this period was the Elizabethan. Then the speech of poetry got into it a ring and turn of direct intuitive power, a spontaneous fullness of vision and divine fashion in its utterance which it had not at all before and has hardly had afterwards. Even the lesser poets of the time are touched by it, but in Shakespeare it runs in a stream or condenses to a richly-loaded and crowding mass of the work and word of the intuition almost unexampled in any poetry. The difference can be measured by taking the work of Chaucer or of subsequent poets almost at their best and of Shakespeare at a quite ordinary level and feeling the effect on the poetic listener in our own intuitive being." Sri Aurobindo takes Chaucer's line—

He was a very parfit gentle knight—

to which for completer comparison with Shakespeare we may add the three other lines of the same passage about that knight's noble deeds:

At mortal batailles hadde he bene fiftene
And foughten for our faith at Tramissene
In listes thryës and ay slain his fo...

Now pass from "Chaucer with his easy adequate limpidity" to "Shakespeare's rapid seizing of the intuitive inevitable word and the disclosing turn of phrase which admits us at once to a direct vision of the thing he shows"—Othello's account of his military life:

> Of moving accidents, by flood and field,
> Of hair-breadth 'scapes i' the imminent deadly breach,
> Of being taken by the insolent foe... (I.iii. 134-136)

There "with quite as simple a thing to say and a perfect force of directness in saying it, it is yet a vastly different kind of directness.... It is not merely a difference of the measure of the genius, but of its source. This language of Shakespeare's is a unique and wonderful thing; it has everywhere the royalty of the sovereign intuitive mind looking into and not merely at life" with a "readiness to get through, seize the lurking word and bring it out from the heart of the thing itself.... We are most readily struck in Shakespeare by the lines and passages in which the word thus seized and brought out is followed swiftly on the heels by another and another of its kind, many crowding together or even fused and run into each other in a single phrase of many suggestions,—for this manner is peculiarly his own and others can only occasionally come near to it. Such passages recur to the mind as those in the soliloquy on sleep [in *2 Henry IV*] or the well-known lines in *Macbeth*,

> Pluck from the memory a rooted sorrow,
> Raze out the written troubles of the brain,
> And with some sweet oblivious antidote
> Cleanse the stuffed bosom of that perilous stuff
> Which weighs upon the heart.[3]

His is often a highly imaged style, but Shakespeare's images are not, as with so many poets, decorative or brought in to enforce and visualise the intellectual sense, they are more immediately revelatory, intimate to the thing he speaks and rather the proper stuff of the fact itself than images. But he has too a clearer, less crowded, still swifter fashion of speech in which they are absent; for an example,

> She should have died hereafter;
> There would have been a time for such a word,—[4]

which has yet the same deep and penetrating intuitive spirit in its utterance. Or the two manners meet together and lean on each other,—

> I have lived long enough: my way of life
> Is fall'n into the sere, the yellow leaf,[5]

or become one, as in the last speeches of Antony,—

> I am dying, Egypt, dying; only
> I here importune death awhile, until
> Of many thousand kisses the poor last
> I lay upon thy lips.[6]

But all have the same characteristic stamp of the intuitive mind rapidly and powerfully at work."[7]

Apropos of the last quotation we may catch a sidelight from Sri Aurobindo on a theme favourite with Matthew Arnold: nobility of style. In a letter to a disciple, discussing this quality in relation to Chapman and Homer, he[8] wrote: "then I come to Arnold's example of which you question the nobility on the strength of my description of one essential of the poetically noble. Mark that the calm, self-mastery, beautiful control which I have spoken of as essential to nobility is a poetic, not an ethical or Yogic calm and control. It does not exclude the poignant expression of grief or passion, but it expresses it with a certain high restraint so that even when the mood is personal it yet borders on the widely impersonal. Cleopatra's words [to the asp]—

> Come, thou mortal wretch,
> With thy sharp teeth this knot intrinsicate
> Of life at once untie; poor venomous fool,
> Be angry, and despatch—[9]

are an example of what I mean; the disdainful compassion for the fury of the chosen instrument of self-destruction which vainly thinks it can truly hurt her, the call to death to act swiftly and yet the sense of being high above what death can do, which these few simple words convey has the true essence of nobility. 'Impatience' only! You have not caught the significance of the words 'poor venomous fool', the tone of the 'Be angry, and despatch', the tense and noble grandeur of the suicide scene with the high light it sheds on Cleopatra's character. For she was a remarkable woman, a great queen, a skilful ruler and politician, not merely the erotic intriguer people make of her. Shakespeare is not good at describing greatness, he poetised the *homme moyen*, but he has caught something here. The whole passage stands on a par with the words of Antony 'I am dying, Egypt, dying' (down to 'A Roman by a Roman valiantly vanquished') which stand among the noblest expressions of high, deep, yet collected and contained emotion in literature—though that is a masculine and this is a feminine nobility."

Here another observation of Sri Aurobindo's becomes appropriate, both because it links up with Antony's death-scene and because it mentions lines which our citation from Sri Aurobindo on Shakespeare's intuitiveness of speech left unquoted—the lines from 2 *Henry IV* to sleep:

> Wilt thou upon the high and giddy mast
> Seal up the ship-boy's eyes, and rock his brains
> In cradle of the rude imperious surge? (III. i. 18-20)

A friend of a disciple had pronounced these lines lax and rhetorical in their richness and to belong to an inferior Shakespearean style. Sri Aurobindo[10] remarked: "X's disparagement...seems to me to illustrate a serious limitation in his poetic perception and temperamental sympathies. Shakespeare's later terse and packed style with its more powerful dramatic effects can surely be admired without disparaging the beauty and opulence of his earlier style; if he had never written in that style, it would have been an unspeakable loss to the sum of the world's aesthetic possessions. The lines...are neither lax nor merely rhetorical, they have a terseness or at least a compactness of their own, different in character from the lines, let us say, in the scene of Antony's death or other memorable passages written in his great tragic style but none the less at every step packed with pregnant meanings and powerful significances which would not be possible if it were merely a loose rhetoric. Anyone writing such lines would deserve to rank by them alone among the great and even the greatest poets."

The same three lines enter also Sri Aurobindo's argument that the greatest lines of poetry have a certain independence of their contexts. He criticises the translators of Virgil who hitch the Mantuan's *lacrimae rerum*, "tears of things", wholly to the immediate reference to distant Carthage sympathising with and weeping over the misfortunes of Troy. According to Sri Aurobindo, Virgil not only rises from a particularity to a universality but also feels a brooding cosmic sense and a profound soul-response and gives the entire pathetic perception an immortal body of the highest inspiration. Sri Aurobindo[11] continues: "Lines like these seldom depend upon their contexts, they rise from it as if a single Himalayan peak from a range of low hills or even from a flat plain. They have to be looked at by themselves, valued for their own sake, felt in their independent greatness. Shakespeare's lines upon sleep—

Wilt thou upon the high and giddy mast
Seal up the ship-boy's eyes, and rock his brains
In cradle of the rude imperious surge?—

depend not at all upon the context which is indeed almost irrelevant, for he branches off into a violent and resonant description of a storm at sea which has its poetic quality, but that quality has something comparatively quite inferior, so that these few lines stand quite apart in their unsurpassable magic and beauty. What has happened is that the sudden wings of a supreme inspiration from above have swooped down upon him and abruptly lifted him for a moment to highest heights, then as abruptly dropped him and left him to his normal resources. One can see him in the lines that follow straining these resources to try and get something equal to the greatness of this light but failing except partly for one line only. Or take those lines in *Hamlet*—

> Absent thee from felicity awhile,
> And in this harsh world draw thy breath in pain...

They arise out of a rapid series of violent melodramatic events but they have quite a different ring from all that surrounds them, however powerful that may be. They come from another plane, shine with another light: the close of the sentence—'To tell my story'—which connects it with the thread of the drama slips down in a quick incline to a lower inspiration. It is not a dramatic interest we feel when we read these lines; their appeal does not arise from the story but would be the same anywhere and in any context. We have passed from the particular to the universal, to a voice from the cosmic self, to a poignant reaction of the soul of man and not of Hamlet alone to the pain and sorrow of this world and its longing for some unknown felicity beyond...."

The lines on sleep, as well as those from *Hamlet*, receive a light on their source and we get a gloss on Sri Aurobindo's turn—"inspiration from above"—in his exposition of what he has designated "overhead poetry". This exposition involves terms like "illumined" and "intuitive", among others, but they have to be distinguished from the epithet "illumined" applied to one of the five styles and the epithet "intuitive" which applies to the essential movement of supreme inspiration on any plane. "The intuitive mind rapidly at work" in Shakespeare is the power that constitutes the sheer inevitability of the last of the five styles. But, like illumination, intuition is part of the "overhead" afflatus in a special and distinct sense relating to a plane of existence.

We have already quoted Sri Aurobindo on "a superconscient source above the ordinary mentality", from which "the impetus to poetic creation comes". The practitioner of the Aurobindonian Integral Yoga becomes aware of this source in general as an immense ether of being, consciousness and bliss, at once static and dynamic, hidden high over the head where the brain-clamped mind of man works. It is this occult spaciousness of living Presence overhead that is ultimately responsible for man's traditional feeling that God exists up above in the sky. Overhead poetry is the rhythmic speech of the several gradations within that spaciousness. It either deals with mystical and spiritual themes with a self-disclosing profundity that seems native to them or else it brings into the treatment of any theme the direct sense of "something behind not belonging to the mind or the vital and physical consciousness and with that a certain quality or power in the language and the rhythm which helps to bring out that deeper something"[12]

The overhead plane nearest to us is the Higher Mind or Higher Thought, next is the Illumined Mind, then the Intuition in its pure form— a form to be psychologically differentiated "from the mental intuition which is frequent enough in poetry that does not transcend the mental level"[13] and which, again, is not the same as the full intuitive power of the soul-mind constituting the sheer inevitability. The highest plane manifest so far in the world's literature is named by Sri Aurobindo the Over-

81

mind, the fount of what in India has been venerated as the *mantra*, the Divine Word whose greatest wingings have been found in the Rig Veda, the Gita and most in the Upanishads. We may quote from Sri Aurobindo[14] brief pointers to the qualities of each of these overhead levels as it proceeds on its mission of overt or covert echo of some infinite beyond the mind.

"The higher thought has a strong tread often with bare unsandalled feet and moves in a clear-cut light: a divine power, measure, dignity is its most frequent character. The outflow of the illumined mind comes in a flood brilliant with revealing words or a light of crowding images, something surcharged with its burden of revelations, sometimes with a luminous sweep. The intuition is usually a lightning flash showing up a single spot or plot of ground or scene with an entire and miraculous completeness of vision to the surprised ecstasy of the inner eye; its rhythm has a decisive inevitable sound which leaves nothing essential unheard, but very commonly is embodied in a single stroke.... The language and rhythm from these other overhead levels can be very different from that which is proper to the Overmind; for the Overmind thinks in a mass; its thought, feeling, vision is high or deep or wide or all these things together: to use the Vedic expression about fire, the divine messenger, it goes vast on its way to bring the divine riches, and it has a corresponding language and rhythm."

Sri Aurobindo[15] continues: "There are...in mental poetry derivations or substitutes for all these styles. Milton's 'grand style' is such a substitute for the manner of the Higher Thought.... Shakespeare's poetry coruscates with a play of the hues of imagination which we may regard as a mental substitute for the inspiration of the illumined mind and sometimes by aiming at an exalted note he links on to the illumined overhead inspiration itself as in the lines I have more than once quoted:

> Wilt thou upon the high and giddy mast
> Seal up the ship-boy's eyes, and rock his brains
> In cradle of the rude imperious surge...?

But the rest of the passage falls away in spite of its high-pitched language and resonant rhythm far below the overhead strain. So it is easy for the mind to mistake and take the higher for the lower inspiration or *vice versa*."

We may cite the rest of the passage to illustrate the contrast:

> And in the visitation of the winds,
> Who take the ruffian billows by the top,
> Curling their monstrous heads, and hanging them
> With deafening clamour in the slippery clouds,
> That with the hurly death itself awakes?

The lines to sleep figure again when Sri Aurobindo is defending the use of a wealth-burdened movement to express certain mystical visions or experiences. His letter[16] runs: "Can't see the validity of any prohibition of double adjectives in abundance.... According to certain canons epithets should be used sparingly, free use of them is rhetorical, an 'obvious' device, a crowding of images is bad taste, there should be subtlety of art not displayed but severely concealed—*Summa ars est celare artem*.[a] Very

a. The highest art is to conceal art.

good for a certain standard of poetry, not so good or not good at all for others. Shakespeare kicks over these traces at every step, Aeschylus freely and frequently, Milton whenever he chooses." Then, quoting three lines of Milton's—

> With hideous ruin and combustion, down
> To bottomless perdition, there to dwell
> In adamantine chains and penal fire—

and the above three of Shakespeare's and asking us to note two double adjectives in the latter example, he tells us that Milton's and Shakespeare's verses here "are not subtle or restrained, or careful to conceal their elements of powerful technique, they show rather a vivid richness or vehemence, forcing language to its utmost power of expression."

Part of the same Shakespearean quotation recurs in answers to a disciple's question whether Sri Aurobindo's own line from *Savitri*—

> Never a rarer creature bore his shaft—[17]

was employing the *r*-effect deliberately. Sri Aurobindo[18] wrote: "Yes, like Shakespeare's

> ...*r*ock his b*r*ains
> In c*r*adle of the *r*ude impe*r*ious su*r*ge.

Mine has only three sonant r's, the others being inaudible —Shakespeare pours himself 5 in a close space."

The final reference to the passage comes in a letter

discussing epic greatness and sublimity in poetic speech. Sri Aurobindo[19] makes the pronouncement: "I don't know how I differentiate between the epic and the other kinds of poetic power. Victor Hugo in the *Légende des Siècles* tries to be epic and often succeeds, perhaps even on the whole. Marlowe is sometimes great or sublime, but I would not call him epic.[a] There is a greatness or sublimity that is epic, there is another that is not epic, but more of a romantic type. Shakespeare's line

> In cradle of the rude imperious surge

is as sublime as anything in Homer or Milton, but it does not seem to me to have the epic ring, while a very simple line can have it, e.g. Homer's

> Bê de kat Oulumpoio karênôn chôömenos kêr

(He went down from the peaks of Olympus wroth at heart)

or Virgil's

> Disce, puer, virtutem ex me verumque laborem,
> Fortunam ex aliis[b]

---

a. Marlowe's "epic" genius discussed elsewhere is a different issue. —K.D.S.

b. From me you may learn courage and what real effort is;
From others, the meaning of fortune. (C. Day Lewis)
Perhaps a more Virgilian accent may be caught by translating:
Learn from me, youth, what is courage and what true labour,
Fortune from others.—K.D.S.

or Milton's

> Fall'n Cherub! to be weak is miserable.

What is there in these lines that is not in Shakespeare's and makes them epic (Shakespeare's of course has something else as valuable)? .... A tone of the inner spirit perhaps, expressing itself in the rhythm and the turn of the language.... Dante has the epic spirit and tone, what he lacks is the epic élan and swiftness. The distinction you draw—'epic sublimity has a more natural turn of imagination than the non-epic: it is powerfully wide or deep or high without being outstandingly bold, it also displays less colour'— applies, no doubt, but I do not know whether it is the essence of the thing or only one result of a certain austerity in the epic Muse. I do not know whether one cannot be coloured provided one keeps that austerity which, be it understood, is not incompatible with a certain fineness and sweetness."

We may add that the line Sri Aurobindo has picked out from Milton for its epic ring returns in another context with another line of Shakespeare's beside it. Now the question is not of the epic style or of austerity in spirit and tone and Sri Aurobindo's observations show the extreme plasticity as well as sensitivity of his response to poetry. He[20] writes: "All poets have lines which are bare and direct statements and meant to be that in order to carry their full force; but to what category their simplicity belongs or whether a line is only passable or more than that depends on various circumstances. Shakespeare's

> To be or not to be, that is the question[21]

introduces powerfully one of the most famous of all soliloquies and it comes in with a great dramatic force, but in itself it is a bare statement and some might say that it would not be otherwise written in prose and is only saved by the metrical rhythm. The same might be said of the well-known passage in Keats:

> Beauty is Truth, Truth Beauty—that is all
> Ye know on earth and all ye need to know.

The same might be said of Milton's famous line,

> Fall'n Cherub! to be weak is miserable.

But obviously in all these lines there is not only a concentrated force, power or greatness of the thought, but also a concentration of intense poetic feeling which makes any criticism impossible."

Hamlet's soliloquy is once more drawn upon by Sri Aurobindo—this time while pointing out the short comings of the conventional critical intellect *vis-à-vis* overhead poetry. "The mere critical intellect not touched by a rarer sight," Sri Aurobindo[22] says, "can do little here. We can take an extreme case, for in extreme cases certain incompatibilities come out more clearly. What might be called the Johnsonian critical method has obviously little or no place in this field,—the method which expects a precise logical order in thoughts and language and pecks at all that departs from a matter-of-fact or a strict and rational ideative coherence or a sober and restrained classical taste.... But also this method is useless in dealing with any kind of romantic poetry. What would the

Johnsonian critic say to Shakespeare's famous lines,

> Or take up arms against a sea of troubles
> And by opposing end them?[a]

He would say, 'What a mixture of metaphors and jumble of ideas! Only a lunatic could take up arms against a sea! A sea of troubles is too fanciful a metaphor and, in any case, one can't end the sea by opposing it, it is more likely to end you.' Shakespeare knew very well what he was doing; he saw the mixture as well as any critic could and he accepted it because it brought home, with an inspired force which a neater language could not have had, the exact feeling and idea that he wanted to bring out."

I may interrupt to add that a proof of Shakespeare's awareness of what he was doing is that he skilfully eludes being caught by the Johnsonian critic's booby-trap: "Can one end a sea instead of being ended by it?" Mark that in the second half-line Shakespeare speaks not of ending the sea but of ending the troubles—he uses 'them' and not 'it'."

To let Sri Aurobindo continue: "Still more scared would the Johnsonian be by any occult or mystic poetry. The Veda, for instance, uses with what seems like a deliberate recklessness the mixture, at least the association of disparate images, of things not associated together in the material world which in Shakespeare is only an occasional departure.... Fortunately here the modernists with all their errors have broken old bounds and the

---

a. III.i. 59-60. Actually the lines start "Or to take arms", not "Or take up arms". I am retaining the form commented on by Sri Aurobindo.—K.D.S.

mystic poet may be more free to invent his own technique."

With this citation from Sri Aurobindo we return to the subject of overhead poetry in particular and mystical-spiritual poetry in general. Sri Aurobindo would scarcely be in sympathy with critics who attribute some kind of mystical experience to Shakespeare of the final plays. Much has been made of Prospero's speech, beginning "Our revels now are ended", going on to the melting of the spirit-actors into "thin air", predicting a similar dissolution of "the great globe itself", as complete as of "the baseless fabric of this vision", "this insubstantial pageant", and concluding with the judgment:

> We are such stuff
> As dreams are made on, and our little life
> Is rounded with a sleep.[23]

I proposed to Sri Aurobindo a reading in which, just as the actor-spirits conjured up by Prospero have not really been destroyed but, while seeming to melt into thin air, have returned to their unknown realm, so also the sleep of death is an annihilation in appearance only and is really an unknown state which is our original mode of existence. I added: "The passage evokes an intuition of some transcendent God-self who experiences through each individual life a dream-interlude of 'insubstantial pageant' between a divine peace and peace. We are reminded of the Upanishad's description of the mystic trance, *samādhi*, in which the whole world fades like an illusion and the individual soul enters the supreme Spirit's unfeatured ecstasy of repose. Shakespeare's intuition is not pure Upanishad, the supreme Spirit is not clearly felt and whatever profundity is there is vague and unintentional: still, a looming mystic light does appear, stay a little, find a suggestive contour before receding and falling away to a music sublimely defunctive."

Sri Aurobindo[24] replied: "I don't think Shakespeare had any such idea in his mind. What he is dwelling on is the insubstantiality of the world and of human existence. 'We are such stuff' does not point to any God-self. 'Dream' and 'sleep' would properly imply Somebody who dreams and sleeps, but the two words are merely metaphors. Shakespeare is not an intellectual or philosophic thinker nor a mystic one. All that you can say is that there comes out here an impression or intimation of the illusion of Maya, the dream-character of life, but without any vision or intimation of what is behind the dream and the illusion. There is nothing in the passage that even hints vaguely the sense of something abiding—all is insubstantial, 'into air, into thin air', 'baseless fabric', 'insubstantial pageant', '*we are such stuff as dreams are made on*'. 'Stuff' points to some inert material rather than a spirit dreamer or sleeper. Of course one can always read things into it for one's own pleasure, but. . . .

"....Shakespeare's idea here as everywhere is the expression of a mood of the vital mind, it is not a reasoned philosophical conclusion. However, if you like to argue that, logically, this or that is the true philosophical consequence of what Shakespeare says and that therefore the Daemon who inspired him must have meant that, I have no objection. I am simply interpreting the passage as Shakespeare's transcribing mind has put it."

I persisted that our interpretation should take stock of the fact that the spirits who contrived the pageant survived it. I quoted what Prospero said to them immediately after they had vanished and also what he said in another part of the play to Ariel when the latter had lured Prospero's enemies into a "foul lake":

> This was well done, my bird.
> Thy shape invisible retain thou still.   (IV.i. 184-185.)

I referred to some stage-directions, too, showing the existence of the spirits. I concluded that only the visible shapes and formations vanished—the entities remained behind all the time and so my idea should be countenanced.

Sri Aurobindo[25] answered: "I don't see what all that has to do with the meaning of the passage in question which plainly insists that nothing endures. Obviously Ariel had an invisible shape—invisible to human eyes, but the point of the passage is that all shapes and substances and beings disappear into nothingness. We are concerned with Prospero's meaning, not with what actually happened to the spirits or for that matter to the pageant in total which we might conceive also of having an invisible source or material. He uses the disappearance of the pageant and the spirits as a base for the idea that all existence is an illusion—it is the idea of the illusion that he enforces. If he had wanted to say, 'We disappear, all disappears to view but the reality of us and of all things persists in a greater immaterial reality', he would surely have said so or at least not left it to be inferred or reasoned out by you in the twentieth century. I repeat, however, that this is my view of Shakespeare's meaning and does not affect any possibility of reading into it something that Shakespeare's outer mind did not receive or else did not express."

Lest we should misunderstand Sri Aurobindo's refusal to see a spiritual visionary in Shakespeare, we must remind ourselves that the idea of world-illusion without any idea of a transcendental substratum could very well be couched in the language and rhythm of the highest spiritual consciousness: Shakespeare had incalculable possibilities of transmitting inspiration. In a comparison of him with Milton on the whole, Sri Aurobindo[26] has said: "Milton's architecture of thought and verse is high and powerful and massive, but there are usually no subtle echoes there, no deep chambers: the occult things in man's being are foreign to his intelligence,—for it is in the light of the poetic intelligence that he works. He does not stray into 'the mystic cavern of the heart'.... Shakespeare does sometimes get in as if by a splendid psychic accident in spite of his preoccupation with the colours and shows of life."

One has to remember that the ostensible subject of a piece of poetry does not put it on the hither or the yonder side of the frontier between the overhead and the usual type of poetic inspiration. Merely by the use of so-called spiritual terms like "eternity" or "heaven" one hardly rises into the spiritual ether. Thus, when I quoted to Sri Aurobindo those verses from *Antony and Cleopatra*—

> Eternity was in our lips and eyes,
> Bliss in our brows bent; none our parts so poor
> But was a race of heaven—   (I.iii. 35-37)

and asked what plane they so magnificently, so idealistically manifested, he[27] replied: "The quotation...is plainly vital in its excited thrill". On the other hand, without any explicit spiritual sense or turn, one could cross the frontier. Sri Aurobindo[28] wrote: "You speak...of the sense of the Infinite and the One which is pervasive in the Overhead planes; that need not be explicitly there in the overhead poetic expression or in the substance of any given line: it can be expressed indeed by overhead poetry as no other can express it, but this poetry can deal with quite other things. I would certainly say that Shakespeare's lines

   Absent thee from felicity awhile,
   And in this harsh world draw thy breath in pain,

have the overhead touch in the substance, the rhythm and the feeling; but Shakespeare is not giving us here the sense of the One and the Infinite. He is, as in the other lines of his which have this note, dealing as he always does with life, with vital emotions and reactions or the thoughts that spring out in the life-mind under the pressure of life."

Even the clear Overmind afflatus Sri Aurobindo has ascribed to Shakespeare. He[29] picks out first—as most suggesting in European literature "an almost direct descent from the overmind consciousness"—the line from the *Aeneid* about what he calls "the touch of tears in mortal things." Then he adds that another might be Shakespeare's

   In the dark backward and abysm of Time.[30]

For a general characterisation of the poetic quality of this phrase we may attend to Sri Aurobindo's description[31] of the *mantra*. "The *mantra* (not necessarily in the Upanishads alone)...is what comes from the Overmind inspiration. Its characteristics are a language that says infinitely more than the mere sense of the words seems to indicate, a rhythm that means even more than the language and is born out of the Infinite and disappears into the Infinite and the power to convey not merely some mental, vital or physical contents or indications or values of the thing it speaks of, but its value and figure in some fundamental and original consciousness which is behind them all."

Elsewhere Sri Aurobindo[32] has spoken of the Cosmic Self and its consciousness as responsible for the Overmind poetry: "things then tend to be seen not as the mind or heart or body sees them but as this greater consciousness feels or sees or answers to them." And then what is behind the mental thought, the vital emotion, the physical sight "is usually forced to the front or close to the front by a combination of words which carries the suggestion of a deeper meaning or by the force of an image or, most of all, by an intonation and a rhythm which carry up the depths in their wide wash or long march or mounting surge". Briefly analysing a verse of Milton's, which too he calls an Overmind inspiration—

Those thoughts that wander through Eternity—

Sri Aurobindo[33] says: "Milton's line lives by its choice of the word 'wander' to collocate with 'through Eternity'; if he had chosen any other word, it would no longer have been an overhead line, even if the surface sense had been exactly the same." If, for instance, we put "travel" instead, we shall have more alliteration but the whole phrase will move less profoundly: vibrations will not be set up in the deep layers of our receptive consciousness.

"Wander" has a plunging resonance which, with "thoughts" before and "through Eternity" after, creates a sense of space on widening space, expanse on expanse of mystery, continuity on endless continuity of conceptual exploration.

"In this technique," writes Sri Aurobindo[34] in relation to an instance of the Overmind inspiration transmitted by a disciple of his, "it must be the right word and no other, in the right place and in no other, the right sounds and no others, in a design of sound that cannot be changed even a little. You may say that it must be so in all poetry; but in ordinary poetry the mind can play about, chop and change, use one image or another, put this word here or that word there—if the sense is much the same and has a poetical value, the mind does not feel that all is lost unless it is very sensitive and much influenced by the solar plexus. In the overhead poetry these things are quite imperative, it is all or nothing—or at least all or a fall."

Perhaps we may illustrate from Shakespeare himself what Sri Aurobindo means by the possibility of the mind playing about in ordinary poetry. We may pick out from Hamlet's soliloquy that line which ends with the same two words as in the Overmind-snatch:

For who would bear the whips and scorns of time...?
(III.i.70)

This is a splendid phrase, accurate in all its components, but it would not receive a fatal wound if "whips" and "scorns" changed places. The collocation "scorns of time" is not inviolable: "abysm of time" absolutely is. Even to say "abyss of time" would take away an overtone necessary to the inner meaning. As in the other line, Shakespeare is not activising concretely an observation of the misfortune suffered in a changing mortal existence such as all of us know: he is catching an awesome impalpable reality in its very essence of strangeness. And the reverberation of the labials cannot be sacrificed: they are indispensable for shaking the soul with fathomless terror, just as the exact words in the opening part of the line are required to combine with suggestiveness a sharpness of impact making us—as L. C. Knights[35] puts it—"momentarily *feel* the giddy horror (as though in danger of falling 'backward') of the abyss that opens when time is considered solely as unending succession and the past, therefore, as infinitely receding."

Another line of Shakespeare's may also be traced to the mantric source. When I culled it from Sonnet 107 and brought it to Sri Aurobindo's notice, he was surprised and wondered what such a phrase was doing in that context. From his comment I gathered that it had an Overmind movement as well as substance coming strongly coloured by the vital consciousness in which Shakespeare was centred. Here is my culling:

the prophetic soul
Of the wide world, dreaming on things to come.   (1-2)

An interesting point to mark is that now too the Overmind utterance carries a marked labial note—"drea*m*ing", "co*m*e"—and the very same labial is at play here as in the other *mantra*. But there seems a little difference between the two voices from the Overmind. The vital plane is nearly submerged in the Overmind's version of the abysm of time, whereas its presence is potent in the analogous version of the world-soul. Sri Aurobindo emphasises its vital vibration by a comparison with a *mantra* from Wordsworth. He[36] says: "it is quite different in tone from Wordsworth's line on Newton—

Voyaging through strange seas of Thought, alone—

which is an above-head vision—and the difference comes because the vision of the 'dreaming soul' is felt through the vital mind and heart before it finds expression."

However, this vision is of exceptional interest. It provides just the factor that was missing in the Prospero-passage. There the world's illusion was gloriously figured, without any inkling of an abiding spiritual reality behind. Here is a phrase which seems to figure precisely such a reality and the word "dream" common to the two utterances appears extremely suggestive. Like the lines about a divinity that shapes our ends, here is the articulation of a superhuman presence and with something of an accent directly from a superhuman plane. Considered by themselves, the words suggest the Cosmic Self whose brooding voice constitutes the *mantra*. But what exactly did Shakespeare have in mind when he threw them into his Sonnet?

The Sonnet has been regarded as alluding to contemporary events: some have dated it to the time of the Spanish Armada's defeat in 1588; others to that of the defeat of the Turks by the Austro-Hungarians in either 1593 or 1594, an event for all-Europe celebration; still others to this or that surmounted crisis in Queen Elizabeth's life during 1594-1601 or else to her death in 1603. All the datings revolve round the interpretation of the line:

The mortal moon hath her eclipse endured...(5)

For, the Armada came in crescent formation, the religious symbol of the Turks was the crescent, Queen Elisabeth was often called Cynthia (the Moon Goddess) because of her proclaimed virginity. But if contemporary events are read in the Sonnet the meaning of our mystic-sounding phrase would become fairly commonplace: it would be a somewhat high-flown pointer to the forebodings of either all Protestants or all Christians or all Englishmen, especially Protestant ones. If a real eclipse of the moon—and there were several such eclipses during the period 1592-1609—is read, the connotation might be enlarged. What it actually was must remain a mystery, particularly as the whole Sonnet is couched in arcane terms. The poem makes the most elusive, the strangest 14 lines Shakespeare ever wrote:

> Not mine own fears, nor the prophetic soul
> Of the wide world, dreaming on things to come
> Can yet the lease of my true love control,
> Supposed as forfeit to a confined doom.
> The mortal moon hath her eclipse endured,
> And the sad augurs mock their own presage;
> Incertainties now crown themselves assured,
> And peace proclaims olives of endless age.
> Now with the drops of this most balmy time,
> My love looks fresh, and Death to me subscribes,
> Since, spite of him, I'll live in this poor rime,
> While he insults o'er dull and speechless tribes;
>   And thou in this shalt find thy monument
>   When tyrants' crests and tombs of brass are spent.

One almost thinks of Housman's definition of "pure

poetry"—poetry that does not convey thought so much as transfuses emotion and is independent of intellectual meaning and consists of a wonderful thoughtless thrill—poetry that goes back to "something in man which is obscure and latent, something older than the present organisation of his nature, like the patches of fen which still linger here and there in the drained lands of Cambridgeshire". Housman does bring in some passages of Shakespeare—paricularly the lyric "Take, O take those lips away"—as instances of pure poetry. But his central exemplar of the pure poet is Blake whom he therefore considers more essentially a poet than even Shakespeare. Well, the Sonnet we have quoted may be best described as strikingly Blakean in a key less complicated than Blake's. Housman does not refer to it, but what can be more illustrative of what he terms as typical of Blake—embryo images and mysterious grandeurs, with nothing evolved, nothing given a definite mental identity? Does it not in its own manner resemble the poem Housman cites from Blake?

> Hear the voice of the Bard,
>   Who present, past and future sees;
> Whose ears have heard
> The Holy Word
>   That walked among the ancient trees.
>
> Calling the lapsèd soul
>   And weeping in the evening dew;
> That might control
> The starry pole,
>   And fallen, fallen light renew.

'O Earth, O Earth, return!
 Arise from out the dewy grass;
Night is worn,
And the morn
 Rises from the slumberous mass.

Turn away no more;
 Why wilt thou turn away?
The starry floor,
The watery shore
 Is given thee till the break of day.'

Even some direct parallels may be picked out. The prophetic soul with its dream of things to come shadows forth the Bard who sees present, past and future. The allusion to the control of true love's lease which is supposed to be forfeit to a confined doom chimes with the mention of the control of the starry pole resulting in a renewal of fallen light. This renewal has also a prefiguration in the mortal moon's endurance of her eclipse. The evening dew and the dewy grass as well as the ancient trees are anticipated by the drops of the most balmy time and olives of endless age. Just as the dewy grass is followed by

Night is worn,
And the morn
 Rises from the slumberous mass,

so also the drops of the most balmy time are followed by

My love looks fresh and Death to me subscribes...

100

The lines after this—

> Since, spite of him, I'll live in this poor rime,
> While he insults o'er dull and speechless tribes—

send us to Blake's "voice of the Bard" and his "Holy Word" on the one hand and on the other to earth's rising "from the slumberous mass", the dull and speechless inertia, as it were, of those who are plunged in a torpid state symbolic of Death. Blake's ending has a vaguer vividness than the Sonnet's; yet the latter's "tombs of brass" have some undefined generality about them, nor can one help asking: "Who are the tyrants and what are their crests?" And the endings of both the poems have a note of combined solace and assurance.

I do not know how Sri Aurobindo would have taken my parallelisms. Perhaps he would have warned me against letting my imagination run too far. But I am certain he would have recognised with me the overall aura of suggestive ambiguity the Sonnet carries. And he has granted also that Shakespeare sometimes by a splendid psychic accident got into the inner chambers of existence, as well as that breaths of the occult could blow through his dramatic genius at rare times, as in *Macbeth* and *Lear*. On the whole, of course, Shakespeare and Blake were geniuses of different orders.

And we may close our survey of Sri Aurobindo on Shakespeare with a few remarks of his apropos of Housman's magnification of Blake over Shakespeare and with Sri Aurobindo's own "prophetic soul"'s pronouncement on poetic "things to come".

5

We read in a letter:[1] "As for Blake and Shakespeare, that opinion is more a personal fantasy than anything else. Purity and greatness are not the same thing; Blake's may be pure poetry in Housman's sense and Shakespeare's not except in a few passages; but nobody can contend that Blake's genius had the width and volume and richness of Shakespeare's. It can be said that Blake as a mystic poet achieved things beyond Shakespeare's measure—for Shakespeare had not the mystic's vision; but as a poet of the play of life Shakespeare is everywhere and Blake nowhere. These are tricks of language and idiosyncrasies of preference. One has to put each thing in its place without confusing issues...."

Here, as everywhere else, we find not only the range, the responsiveness, the insight but also the poise of Sri Aurobindo the literary critic. And a final instance of all these qualities may be given by a reference to what he calls the Future Poetry. If the ultimate fount of inspiration is the Cosmic Self and the Transcendent Spirit, the poetic impulse is bound to press towards the inmost and the upmost and reveal the mystical and spiritual truth in its own sheer form as well as through all the figures of its earthly manifestation. Blake thus is a guide-post in general to the poetry of the future. Not that mystical-spiritual truth need be expressed invariably through a pure poetry such as Housman defines or by means of a semi-Surrealist vision, a baffling Symbolist pattern of language. In Sri Aurobindo's view, there can be a colossal clarity of spiritual sunlight no less than a crowded secrecy of mystical moonlight. But in either of them it is an eye deeper than the Shakespearean that has to be at work, although with a "width and volume and richness" equal to the Shakespearean. Nor are these attributes from Shakespeare the sole ones which Sri Aurobindo considers essential to poetry in an all-fulfilling synthesis of its powers. A *sine qua non* is Shakespeare's intuitive mode of speech, his seizing of the word from the very heart of the thing seen. English poetry after him, by getting intellectualised, lost much of this mode, though in Milton it gained a more dynamic amplitude of imaginative thought as distinguished from imaginative sensation and emotion. The later Romantics have often a clear, strong, large and luninous manner, but by functioning from the more deliberative mental rather than the more spontaneous vital plane they too lack comparatively in "the searching audacities of the intuition". Still, now and then, there emerges, as Sri Aurobindo[2] puts it, "a certain effort to recapture the Shakespearean potency and intensity accompanied by a new and higher element in the workings of the poetic inspiration. When we try to put a name on it...we can see that this is an attempt to return to the fullness and the awakening turn of the direct intuitive expression on a subtler and more ethereal level. The clarified intellect observing life from above is in itself a higher thing than the vital and emotional mind which responds more immediately and powerfully to life, but is caught in its bonds; and if the direct intuitive power can be got to work on the level just above the ordinary thinking mind where that mind opens...to a greater supra-intellectual mass and subtlety of light, it will bring in the revelation and inspiration of mightier and profounder things than when it works from behind the mind—even the vividly thinking mind of life and its vital sight and feeling." Of this effort and this new thing Sri Aurobindo discerns magical first indications in the pre-Victorian poets, as in Wordsworth's

> And beauty born of murmuring sound
> Shall pass into her face,

and, less often, a sudden springing out of the thing itself—

> The journey homeward to habitual self,

or

> ...solitary thinkings such as dodge
> Conception to the very bourne of heaven,
> Then leave the naked brain.

"These lines of Keats," Sri Aurobindo[3] observes, "are Shakespearean in their quality, they have recovered the direct revealing word and intimate image of the full intuitive manner, but they enter into a world of thought and inner truth other than Shakespeare's; by the passage through the detaching intellect and beyond it they have got to the borders of the realm of another and greater self than the life-self, though there we include and take up life into the deeper self-vision."

In the Victorian poets too Sri Aurobindo discovers occasionally the same tendency. But later work wafts it more abundantly to his ear. Thus it is there in Meredith:

for instance, "when he writes,...

> Nor know they joy of sight
> Who deem the wave of rapt desire must be
> Its wrecking and last issue of delight,

he has got the perfected turn of the direct intuitive word of thought in its more crowded manner of suggestion,—the kinship in the last line to the Shakespearean manner is close,—as too its more clear and limpid speech in other turns,

> The song seraphically free
> Of taint of personality:

and in the lines,

> Dead seasons quicken in one petal spot
> Of colour unforgot,

he has it ready for an intuitive and vivid spiritual interpretation of Nature... In the Irish poets it comes with less of the Shakespearean kinship, though Yeats has often enough a different corresponding manner, but most characteristically in a delicate and fine beauty of the word of vision and of an intuitive entrance into the mystery of things...."[4] Sri Aurobindo[5] hears a spiritual intonation attaining its fullness either without any expenditure of device, as in AE's—

> Like winds and waters were her ways:
> They heed not immemorial cries;
> They move to their high destinies
> Beyond the little voice that prays—

105

or with a richer, more colourfully suggestive form, as in a blank verse of Yeats—

A sweet miraculous terrifying sound,

or else with a phrase, again of Yeats, at once simple and loaded—

When God goes by with white footfall.

Sri Aurobindo[6] comments: "This is a style and substance which recovers something that had been lost and yet is new and pregnant of new things in English literature."

Here a brief digression should be in order. We have to mention that moulder of modern free verse and harmonist of modern freedom, Whitman, who is also a pioneer of the future. In one place, Sri Aurobindo[7] calls him "the most Homeric voice since Homer" because of a "nearness to something elemental" which gives "a ring of greatness" and "an air of divinity" to everything he says, and because of an elemental "power of sufficient straighforward speech" with a "rush too of oceanic sound". In another place, Sri Aurobindo[8] says that he has "a robust closeness to the very spirit of life,...more than any other poet since Shakespeare". However, this "almost primitive force of vitality" is "ennobled by a lifting up of its earthly vigour into a broad and full intellectual freedom".[9] In him "thought leads and all is made subject and object and substance of a free and a powerful thinking, but this insistence of thought is made one with the pulse of life and the grave reflective pallor and want of blood of an overburdened intellectualism is healed by that vigorous union". He is also a-thrill with the spirit of modernism: no other writer of the time is so representative a voice of the age, with a large and definite consciousness of the work he had to do—the utterance of the "simple separate person" and yet of "the word Democratic, the word En Masse" and of all Life as one passion, one power and of mankind in tune with universal Nature in a vast web of thought and action. But "Whitman, by the intensity of his intellectual and vital dwelling on the things he saw and expressed, arrives at some first profound sense of....That which the old Indian seers called the *mahān ātmā*, the Great Self, the Great Spirit, which is seen through the vast strain of the cosmic thought and the cosmic life".[10]

The passages, which bring out "the divinity of the soul in man and its kinship to the divinity of the Eternal", "send forward an arc-light of prophetic expression on what is at the very heart of the new movement of humanity".[11] But Whitman's "language and method are still that of the poetic intellect straining to some fullest power of its intelligence and speech-force".[12] Further, the grand total of his work falls short of what, with his Homeric and Shakespearean qualities, he might have achieved. This is due not only to something unrestrained or titanic in him. It is due also to the medium he made his own: free verse.

At his greatest, according to Sri Aurobindo's multi-lingual ear, he arrives consciously or unconsciously at a secret principle which "is the essential principle of Greek choric and dithyrambic poetry turned to the law of a language which has not the strong resource of quantity."[13] "When he gives us the dactylic and spondaic harmony of his lines,

107

> Out of the cradle endlessly rocking,
> Out of the mocking-bird's throat, the musical shuttle,
> Out of the ninth-month midnight,

one of them wanting only one foot to be a very perfect hexameter, or the subtly varied movement of the other passage,

> Over the hoarse surging of the sea,
> Or flitting from brier to brier by day,
> I saw, I heard at intervals the remaining one, the he-bird,
> The solitary guest from Alabama,

one has almost the rhythmical illusion of listening to a Sophoclean or Aeschylean chorus."[14]

"The poetic principle of measure in its essence without the limitations of a set form"[15]—there we have the fount of the natural high-water mark of free verse. It is a formula by which intrinsic quantity, the time taken by the voice over the vowel of a syllable, acquires in English a legitimate place in foot-building, though not in slavish imitation of old rules. A true English quantitative rhythm, says Sri Aurobindo, would be constituted by (1) intrinsic *unstressed* longs acting on an equal basis with the stress and combining with intrinsic shorts to build many-syllabled feet more varying than in Greek or Latin; (2) the stress, which can never be ignored in English, being taken as automatically creating quantitative length by a vertical as opposed to a horizontal mass of voice, even if the stroke falls on an intrinsic short; (3) intrinsic shorts, when unstressed, assuming no length—except on rare occasions—by the mere accumulation of consonants after them. Sri Aurobindo holds that all English speech has a subtle quantitative rhythm, however loose, and that literary prose lifts it to a higher level, whose best and most concentrated examples can be found in Shakespeare and the Bible. He takes a well-known snatch of prose from *Hamlet* and shows how the law of quantitative rhythm, arranges the word-movement:

This goodly frame, | the earth, seems to | me a sterile | promontory; | this most excel|lent canopy, | the air, | look you, | this brave o'erhang|ing firmament, | this majesti|cal roof fretted | with golden fire, | —why, it appears | to me no oth|er thing than a | foul and pesti|lent congrega|tion of vapours. | What a piece of | work is a man! | How noble in | reason, | how infinite | in faculty; | in form, | in moving | how express and | admirable! | in action how | like an angel! | in apprehension | how like a god! | the beauty of | | the world! | the paragon | of animals. | And yet, to me, | what is this quint|essence of dust? | (II.ii.)

"The measures of this prose rhythm," says Sri Aurobindo[16] in a general comment on such passages, "find their units of order in word-groups and not as in poetry in metrical lines; the syllabic combinations which we call feet do not follow here any fixed sequence." Sri Aurobindo[17] also sees a dominant rhythm, which gives an underlying unity to each *ensemble*: "In the instance taken from Shakespeare a remarkable persistence of four-foot measures, with occasional shorter ones intervening, builds up a grave and massive rhythmic feeling and imparts even a poetic motion to the unified whole."

Free verse should raise to their acme the characteristics of this kind of writing. But the acme cannot be reached without an openly accepted discipline to keep the true principle at work. Whitman, like all *vers-libristes*, lacks in that discipline, and the result is that fluctuations of rhythmic intensity become an inherent part of the form. In Sri Aurobindo's judgment,[18] Whitman "is a great poet, one of the greatest in the power of his substance, the energy of his vision, the force of his style, the largeness at once of his personality and his universality". But, apart from shortcomings in psychological make-up, apart from the want of that "self-restraint and obedience to a divine law which makes even the gods more divine",[19] we miss to a certain extent even in his choric or dithyrambic movements the subtler uplift of the poetic enthusiasm which is given by the metrical cadence: "even his greatest things do not go absolutely and immediately home, or having entered they do not so easily seize on the soul, take possession and rest in a calm, yet vibrating mastery."[20]

Free verse, no doubt, indicates a real need of the time, but it must discover its true mode and method and not sacrifice "the intensity of rhythm, which is poetry's primal need"[21] and by whose lowering the two other intensities—that of thought and soul-substance and that of expression—suffer: "the poet himself tends to loosen them to the level of his movement."[22] So, "if the new age is to express itself with the highest poetical power, it must be by a new discovery within the principle of the intenser poetical rhythm"; and "the ordered measures of the poetic spirit, *chhandas*"[23] cannot be ousted by free verse.

To appreciate the difference between the top reach of Whitmanian free verse and the top reach of the older "ordered measures" we need only make two cullings from Whitman at his best and place them alongside a couple of unforgettable moments of Shakespeare. From stanza XIV of *When Lilacs Last in the Dooryard Bloomed*, we may quote the lines, in some of which, according to Sri Aurobindo,[24] Whitman's "attempt at perfection of rhythm...rises to a high-strung acuteness which gives a great beauty of movement":

> Come, lovely and soothing death,
> Undulate round the world, serenely arriving, arriving,
> In the day, in the night, to all, to each,
> Sooner or later delicate death.
> Prais'd be the fathomless universe,
> For life and joy, and for objects and knowledge curious,
> And for love, sweet love—but praise! praise! praise!
> For the sure-enwinding arms of cool-enfolding death....
> Approach, strong deliveress,
> When it is so, when thou hast taken them I joyously sing the dead,
> Lost in the loving floating ocean of thee,
> Laved in the flood by thy bliss, O death.
> From me to thee glad serenades,
> Dances for thee I propose saluting thee, adornments and feastings for thee,
> And the sights of the open landscape and the high-spread sky are fitting,
> And life and the fields, and the huge and thoughtful night.

Now let us watch Shakespeare in an early drama, *Romeo*

and Juliet, trying out the potentialities of blank verse in tragic lyricism. Romeo is in the vault, desperate beside Juliet's body drugged into semblance of death:

> O my love! my wife!
> Death, that hath sucked the honey of thy breath,
> Hath had no power yet upon thy beauty:
> Thou art not conquered; beauty's ensign yet
> Is crimson in thy lips and in thy cheeks,
> And death's pale flag is not advancèd there...
> Why art thou yet so fair? Shall I believe
> That unsubstantial death is amorous,
> And that the lean abhorrèd monster keeps
> Thee here in dark to be his paramour?
> For fear of that I still will stay with thee,
> And never from this palace of dim night
> Depart again: here, here will I remain
> With worms that are thy chambermaids; O! here
> Will I set up my everlasting rest,
> And shake the yoke of inauspicious stars
> From this world-wearied flesh.... (V. iii. 91-96, 102-112)

We may dub Romeo's soliloquy youthful romanticism and find Whitman's apostrophe deeper in vision, but how easily the supreme aesthetic effect is accomplished by the sustained metrical winging of the words in the former!

Let us take Whitman in a passage about which Sri Aurobindo[25] has said: "one of the seers of old time reborn in ours might so have expressed himself in a modern and intellectualised language":

> Greater than stars or suns,
> Bounding, O soul, thou journeyest forth:
> What love than thine and ours could wider amplify?

> What aspirations, wishes outvie thine and ours, O soul?
> What dreams of the ideal? what plans of purity, perfection,
> strength?
> What cheerful willingness for others' sake to give up all?
> For others' sake to suffer all?
> Reckoning ahead, O soul, when thou, the time achieved...
> Surrounded, copest, frontest God, yieldest, the aim attained,
> As filled with friendship, love complete, the Elder Brother
> found,
> The Younger melts in fondness in his arms.

The seeing, the feeling are admirable. But prose dogs their poetry again and again, even if it be the prose of a prophet. And, when the spiritually stirred language soars up free of the prose gravitation, can it match as sheer aesthetic revelation the afflatus meeting our inner ear in the lines that precede Prospero's statement: "We are such stuff/ As dreams are made on..." ? These lines, also "reckoning ahead" and dealing in their own way with "the time achieved", arise as a descriptive generalisation from the end of the magic masque Prospero has conjured up:

> Our revels now are ended. These our actors,
> As I foretold you, were all spirits and
> Are melted into air, into thin air:
> And, like the baseless fabric of this vision,
> The cloud-capped towers, the gorgeous palaces,
> The solemn temples, the great globe itself,
> Yea, all which it inherit, shall dissolve
> And, like this insubstantial pageant faded,
> Leave not a rack behind....   (IV. i. 148-56)

Paradoxically, these lines that swell to a quietly powerful diapason of nihilism not only take swifter possession of the poetic soul of the reader than Whitman's semi-Upanishadic affirmation and rest within it in a calm yet vibrating mastery: they also touch on the pinions of a rhythmic intensity, added to the intensities of vision and word, the overhead level without any open mystical message.

If the overhead level is the final goal of poetry and the promise of the future, experiments in the received ways of word-music rather than in the fluctuant modes of free verse are more likely to compass it. But some conscious recognition of what the future demands is required. Possibly, resurgent India, using English as a sort of second mother-tongue, is more apt to answer the call. But in England itself the turn of intuitive speech towards the in-world and the over-world is already present, even though it is one strand out of many and "the full idea of that thing, the large and clearly conceived substance of thought and vision which should fill this mould of intuitive utterance, we do not get in any considerable degree or range".[26]

In some of the lines of a slightly earlier poet, Meredith, Sri Aurobindo finds a description which might well be applied to the whole drift and cause of the spiritual principle of sight and rhythm, towards which the evolution of poetry is tending. Meredith is speaking of "Colour, the Soul's Bridegroom", leading

> Through widening chambers of surprise to where
> Throbs rapture near an end that aye recedes,
> Because his touch is infinite and lends
> A yonder to all ends.

Perhaps the most telling disclosure as well as exemplar of what the Future Poetry has to express, taking us to greater realities than Shakespeare saw or bodied forth yet developing in its fashion of sight and sound the essential Shakespearean leap of intuitive word—perhaps the most telling exemplar no less than disclosure may be found in the blank verse of Sri Aurobindo's own *Savitri*. In one passage we are told of the work of Inspiration, the lightning-footed goddess, "a sudden messenger from the all-seeing tops":

> In darkness' core she dug out wells of light,
> On the undiscovered depths imposed a form,
> Lent a vibrant cry to the unuttered vasts,
> And through great shoreless, voiceless, starless breadths
> Bore earthward fragments of revealing thought
> Hewn from the silence of the Ineffable.[27]

Or we learn what the seer-poets do when the afflatus of "intuitive knowledge" sweeps through their profundities of consciousness:

> Hearing the subtle voice that clothes the heavens,
> Carrying the splendour that has lit the suns,
> They sang Infinity's names and deathless powers
> In metres that reflect the moving worlds,
> Sight's sound-waves breaking from the soul's great deeps.[28]

In spiritual terms proper to the future that Sri Aurobindo seeks to create, the last line—a *mantra* about the *mantra*—sums up the secret heart of the revelatory energy whose most godlike outflow in secular terms in the past was Shakespeare.

APPENDIX

Sri Aurobindo's earliest writing on Shakespeare dates back to his eighteenth year but it has not survived. We learn of it from a letter by the young Aurobindo, then a student at King's College, Cambridge, to his father in Bengal. The letter, dated 2nd December 1890, mentions a meeting with "the great O. B. otherwise Oscar Browning, who is the feature *par excellence* of King's" and cites among other compliments his remark on an essay by Aurobindo: "It was wonderful." The letter goes on to say: "In this essay (a comparison between Shakespeare and Milton), I indulged my oriental tastes to the top of their bent, it overflowed with rich and tropical imagery, it abounded in antitheses and epigrams and it expressed my real feelings without restraint or reservation. I thought myself that it was the best thing I had ever done, but at school it would have been considered as extraordinarily Asiatic and bombastic."

A late passage on Shakespeare which remained unnoticed when the book was written is rather apt now in the context of the young Aurobindo's "Asiatic" treatment of the Bard. For now the Yogi Sri Aurobindo[1] is dealing with his own Asiatic country's architecture in the course of his defence of Indian culture against the egregious Mr. Archer who defamed it in a book of the early twentieth century by looking at it through distorting foreign spectacles. Sri Aurobindo, writing of the basic Indian vision which starts with an intuition of the single Self behind and within the cosmic manyness, applies it to Indian architecture, especially that of the South. He calls this architec-

1. *The Foundations of Indian Culture* (Sri Aurobindo Birth Centenary Library, Pondicherry 1970), pp. 219-220.

ture "an aesthetic interpretation or suggestion of the one spiritual experience, one in all its complexity and diversity, which founds the unity of the infinite variations of Indian spirituality and religious feeling and the realised union of the human self with the Divine." Then he continues:

"When we look on the multiplicity of the world, it is only a crowded plurality that we can find and to arrive at unity we have to reduce, to suppress what we have seen or sparingly select a few indications or to be satisfied with the unity of this or that separate idea, experience or imagination; but when we have realised the Self, the infinite unity and look back on the multiplicity of the world, then we find that oneness able to bear all the infinity of variation and circumstance we can crowd into it and its unity remains unabridged by even the most endless self-multiplication of its informing creation. We find the same thing in looking at this architecture. The wealth of ornament, detail, circumstance in Indian temples represents the infinite variety and repetition of the worlds,—not our world only, but all the planes,—suggests the infinite multiplicity in the infinite oneness. It is a matter of our own experience and fullness of vision how much we leave out or bring in, whether we express so much or so little or attempt as in the Dravidian style to give the impression of a teeming inexhaustible plenitude. The largeness of this unity is base and continent enough for any super-structure or content of multitude.

"To condemn this abundance as barbarous is to apply a foreign standard. Where after all are we bound to draw the line? To the pure classical taste Shakespeare's art once appeared great but barbarous for a similar reason,—one remembers the Gallic description of him as a drunken barbarian of genius,—his artistic unity non-existent or spoilt by crowding tropical vegetation of incident and character, his teeming imaginations violent, exaggerated, sometimes bizarre, monstrous, without symmetry, proportion and all the other lucid unities, lightnesses, graces loved by the classic mind. That mind might say of his work in language like Mr. Archer's that here there is indeed a titanic genius, a mass of power, but of unity, clarity, classic nobility no trace, but rather an entire absence of lucid grace and lightness and restraint, a profusion of wild ornament and an imaginative riot without law or measure, strained figures, distorted positions and gestures, no dignity, no fine, just, rationally natural and beautiful classic movement and pose. But even the strictest Latin mind has now got over its objections to the 'splendid barbarism' of Shakespeare and can understand that here is a fuller, less sparing and exiguous vision of life, a greater intuitive unity than the formal unities of the classic aesthesis. But the Indian vision of the world and existence was vaster and fuller than Shakespeare's, because it embraced not merely life, but all being, not merely humanity, but all the worlds and all Nature and cosmos. The European mind not having arrived except in individuals at any close, direct, insistent realisation of the unity of the infinite Self or the cosmic consciousness peopled with its infinite multiplicity, is not driven to express these things, cannot understand or put up with them when they are expressed in this oriental art, speech and style and object to it as the Latin mind once objected to Shakespeare. Perhaps the day is not distant when it will see and understand and perhaps even itself try to express the same things in another language."

REFERENCES

CHAPTER 1

1. *Last Poems* (Pondicherry, 1952), p. 5.
2. *Sonnet* 147.13-14.
3. *Ibid.*, 26.1.
4. *Ibid.*, 50.1.
5. *Ibid.*, 97.3.
6. *Ibid.*, 19.1.
7. *Ibid.*, 13.12.
8. *Ibid.*, 19.13-14.
9. *Ibid.*, 81.5.
10. *Ibid.*, 146.11.
11. *Ibid.*
12. *Ibid.*, 104.1.
13. *Ibid.*, 110.12.
14. *Op. cit.*, p. 27.
15. *Savitri*, followed by the Author's Letters on the Poem (Pondicherry, 1954), Book II, Canto 15, p. 341.
16. *The Future Poetry* (Pondicherry, 1953), pp. 8-9, 10.
17. *Letters of Sri Aurobindo*—Third Series: On Poetry and Literature (Bombay, 1949), pp. 301-303.
18. *Ibid.*, p. 302.
19. *Ibid.*, pp. 305-6.
20. *Ibid.*, p. 306.
21. *Ibid.*, pp. 277-78.
22. *Ibid.*, p. 278.
23. *Explorations* (Penguin Books, Harmondsworth, 1964), p. 63.
24. "Shakespeare's Sonnets", *The Listener*, July 2, 1964, p. 9, col. 1.
25. *Letters*, p. 16.
26. *Letters*, pp. 138-9.
27. *Ibid.*, pp. 113-4.
28. *Ibid.*, p. 14.
29. *Correspondence with Sri Aurobindo*—Second Series, by Nirodbaran (Pondicherry, 1959), pp. 204-5.

30. *Sonnet* 86.9.
31. *As You Like It*, III, iii.
32. *Collected Poems* (Pondicherry, 1972), "On Quantitative Metre", pp. 350-52.
33. *As They Liked It* (Harper Torchbooks, 1961), p. 167.
34. *Shakespeare: His World and His Art* (Bombay, 1964), p. 679.
35. *The Future Poetry*, pp. 110-11.
36. *Ibid.*, p. 110.
37. *Ibid.*
38. *Ibid.*, pp. 100-01
39. *Ibid.*, p. 101.

CHAPTER 2

1. *The Future Poetry*, p. 236.
2. *Ibid.*, p. 126.
3. *Ibid.*, pp. 48-9.
4. *Ibid.*, p. 268.
5. *Ibid.*, p. 391.
6. *Life, Literature, Yoga*: Some Letters of Sri Aurobindo (Pondicherry, 1952), p. 31.
7. *The Future Poetry*, pp. 40-1.
8. *Mother India*, August, 1954, p. 52.
9. *Sonnet* 1.1-2.
10. *The Shakespearean Moment* (New York, 1960), p. 39.
11. *Ibid.*, p. 36. fn. 1.
12. *Ibid.*, p. 12.
13. *Life, Literature, Yoga*, p. 94.
14. *The Future Poetry*, pp. 62, 63.
15. *Ibid.*, pp. 159-60.
16. *Kalidasa* (Pondicherry, 1929), p. 14.
17. *Kalidasa*: Second Series (Pondicherry, 1954), p. 71.
18. *Ibid.*, p. 62.
19. *Ibid.*, pp. 62-63.
20. *Ibid.*, pp. 75-76.
21. *Ibid.*, p. 76.
22. *Ibid.*, pp. 38-40.

23. *Twelfth Night*, I.v. 278-284.
24. *Ibid.*, 298-301.
25. *Kalidasa*: Second Series, pp. 11-12.
26. *Ibid.*, pp. 13-14.
27. *Correspondence*, Second Series, p. 215.
28. *Letters*, pp. 202-3.
29. *Kalidasa*: Second Series, p. 17.
30. *Ibid.*, p. 16.
31. *The Future Poetry*, p. 54.
32. *Ibid.*, pp. 58-59.
33. *Ibid.*, pp. 65-66.
34. *Ibid.*, p. 71.
35. *Ibid.*, p. 68. *Cf.*
36. *Letters*, pp. 166-167.
37. *The Future Poetry*, p. 68.
38. *Vyasa and Valmiki* (Pondicherry, 1956), pp. 25-26.
39. *Ibid.*, p. 27.
40. *Savitri*, Book 4, Canto 4, p. 437.
41. *Vyasa and Valmiki*, pp. 69-71.
42. Part 2, III. ii. 233-235.
43. V. iii. 217-220.
44. III. ii. 81-82.
45. IV. xiii. 18-21.
46. *Kalidasa*, p. 27.
47. *Ibid.*
48. *The Future Poetry*, p. 98.

CHAPTER 3

1. *The Future Poetry*, pp. 93-94.
2. *Ibid.*, pp. 94-95.
3. *III. ii.*
4. *The Future Poetry*, p. 324.
5. *Ibid.*, p. 88.
6. *The Future Poetry*, p. 374.
7. *Ibid.*, p. 88.
8. *Ibid.*

9. *Ibid.*, pp. 98-99.
10. *Ibid.*, p. 99.
11. *Ibid.*, pp. 99-100.
12. *Ibid.*, p. 102:
13. *Ibid.*, p. 148.
14. *Ibid.*
15. *Ibid.*, p. 150.
16. *Ibid.*
17. *Ibid.*, p. 147.
18. *Ibid.*, p. 148.
19. *Ibid.*, pp. 148-9.
20. *Ibid.*, p. 199.
21. *Ibid.*, pp. 200-01.
22. *Ibid.*, p. 201.
23. *Ibid.*, pp. 102-03.
24. *Ibid.*, p. 96.

Chapter 4

1. *The Future Poetry*, pp. 236-38.
2. *Ibid.*, p. 238.
3. V. iii. 41-44
4. V. iv. 17-18.
5. V. iii. 22-23.
6. IV. xiii. 18-21.
7. *Ibid.*, pp. 238, 239, 240.
8. *Letters*, pp. 31-32.
9. V. ii. 305-307.
10. *Life, Literature, Yoga*, p. 54.
11. *Ibid.*, pp. 105-6.
12. *Letters*, p. 109.
13. *Ibid.*, p. 116.
14. *Ibid.*, pp. 116-17.
15. *Ibid.*, pp. 117-18.
16. *Savitri*, Letters, pp. 852-3.
17. *Savitri*, Book I, Canto 2, p. 18.
18. *Ibid.*, Letters, p. 862.

19. *Letters*, pp. 26-28.
20. *Savitri*, Letters, p. 863.
21. *Hamlet*, III. i. 56.
22. *Savitri*, Letters, pp. 844-5.
23. *The Tempest*, IV. i. 156-158.
24. *Life, Literature, Yoga*, pp. 108-9, 110.
25. *Ibid.*, p. 111.
26. *Letters*, pp. 118-19.
27. *Life, Literature, Yoga*, p. 31.
28. *Letters*, p. 108.
29. *Ibid.*, p. 109.
30. *The Tempest*, I. ii. 50.
31. *Letters*, p. 97.
32. *Ibid.*, p. 112.
33. *Ibid.*, p. 114.
34. *Ibid.*, p. 94.
35. *Op. cit.*, p. 91, fn. 1.
36. *Life, Literature, Yoga*, p. 32.

CHAPTER 5

1. *Letters*, p. 271.
2. *The Future Poetry*, pp. 242-43.
3. *Ibid.*, p. 244.
4. *Ibid.*, pp. 245-246.
5. *Ibid.*, pp. 233, 234, 246.
6. *Ibid.*, p. 246.
7. *Ibid.*, p. 212.
8. *Ibid.*, p. 253.
9. *Ibid.*
10. *Ibid.*, pp. 254-55.
11. *Ibid.*, p. 257.
12. *Ibid.*
13. *Ibid.*, pp. 214-15.
14. *Ibid.*, p. 215.
15. *Ibid.*, p. 216.
16. *Collected Poems*, "On Quantitative Metre", p. 367.

17. *Ibid.*
18. *The Future Poetry*, p. 212.
19. *Ibid.*
20. *Ibid.*, p. 219.
21. *Ibid.*, p. 220.
22. *Ibid.*
23. *Ibid.*, p. 217.
24. *Collected Poems*, p. 372.
25. *The Future Poetry*, p. 257.
26. *Ibid.*, p. 258.
27. *Savitri*, Book I, Canto 3, p. 48.
28. *Ibid.*, Book IV, Canto 4, p. 435.